Praise for *Hump*

"Hot and hopeful, *Hump* shows ... s-
sible, but a beautiful thing to be ... on
every tired mommy's night star ...
— ... *f Me*

"Written with honesty, style, and wit—Ford's stories assure ... life-
time of passionate humping can be ours!"
—Brett Paesel, author of *Mommies Who Drink:
Sex, Drugs, and Other Distant Memories of an Ordinary Mom*

"Hide it where the kids won't find it! This bawdy memoir, written by a
self-described 'pro-sex' mom, is what every parent needs to spice up the
daily dose of diaper changing and drool. A celebration of sex in the context of marriage, Ford's *Hump* will inspire more adult playtime and
greater intimacy with your spouse."
—Jennifer Margulis, author of *Why Babies Do That*

"Racy, fun, and intelligent, this book should be required reading for new
parents. It's a sure-cure for even the worst case of wilted libido."
—Cindy La Ferle, award-winning journalist
and author of *Writing Home*

"*Hump* is like an invitation to the circle of friends every mother needs . . .
the women who make her feel safe, challenged, respected, and most of
all, entertained."
—Martha Brockenbrough, author of *It Could Happen to You:
Diary of a Pregnancy and Beyond*

"Finally a book about sex after children that isn't a saccharine, maudlin
mess."   —Pepper Schwartz, author of *Prime: Adventures and Advice
on Sex, Love, and the Sensual Years*

"Blunt and funny, *Hump* is California-Kim's definitive antidote to postpartum depression, detailing the frankly explicit solo and partnered
thrills of sex. She invites us to appreciate her evidence: our reproductive
imperative enhances rather than impedes healthy genital friction."
—Lynn Margulis, Distinguished University professor, University of
Massachusetts-Amherst, Department of Geosciences, coauthor with
Dorion Sagan of *Mystery Dance: On the Evolution of Human Sexuality*

HUMP

HUMP

True Tales of Sex After Kids

KIMBERLY FORD

ST. MARTIN'S GRIFFIN
NEW YORK

Author's Note: The events described in these stories are real.
Certain characters have fictitious names and identifying
characteristics.

www.stmartins.com

"Kinderotics" and "Talk to Me, Babies" were first published,
in slightly different forms, in *Brain, Child* magazine.

Book design by Mary A. Wirth

LIBRARY OF CONGRESS CATALOGING-IN-PUBLICATION DATA

Ford, Kimberly.
    Hump : true tales of sex after kids / Kimberly Ford.—1st ed.
        p. cm.
    ISBN-13: 978-0-312-37682-6
    ISBN-10: 0-312-37682-0
    1. Sex in marriage. 2. Intimacy (Psychology) 3. Parents—
Psychology. 4. Married people—Psychology. I. Title.
    HQ728.F64 2008
    646.7'8—dc22   2008012387

First Edition: July 2008

10 9 8 7 6 5 4 3 2 1

For Bill

CONTENTS

Renaissance: An Introduction   1

I. THE HUMP

1. Back in the Saddle   13
2. Kinderotics   31
3. Utility Drawer   45
4. Arguments Against   57

II. STICKY BUSINESS

5. These Are Our Bodies?! These Are Ourselves?! 65
6. Secrets of the Magic Wand   72
7. Talk to Me, Babies   81
8. Arguments Against   93
9. I Touch Myself   95
10. Laser Lover   113
11. Arguments Against   123

III. UP AND OVER

12. Porn Wars   127
13. Snip!   139
14. Snap!   158
15. Pleasure Party   180
16. Arguments Against   205

IV. THE BACKSIDE

17. Viva Las Vegas!   209
18. Arguments Against   229
19. Jealousy   231
20. Into the Sunset   247

    The End: A Conclusion (of Sorts)   265
    Useful Resources   273
    Acknowledgments   275

HUMP

Renaissance:
An Introduction

I love the word fuck. I love its force and versatility. When I labored for thirty hours, pushed for four and a half, then had a C-section, my husband, Bill, tells me I was not shy about using my favorite expletive even with my parents and the venerable Dr. Baldwin in the room.

During the year or so that our son Lucas was preverbal, I felt little need to refrain. I used fuck liberally. A good angry "Fuck!" or a contemplative "Fuuuck . . ." here or there satisfied my sudden need to preserve the youth and vitality that diaper bags and nursing bras threatened.

One sunny afternoon in the tiny kitchen in our first house in Oakland, though, I was trying to stave off the stultifying tedium that came from ten hours alone with my toddler. I was going to treat myself to an old comfort: a huge bowl of Grape-Nuts with half-and-half and copious spoonfuls of sugar. The bowl slipped. Zillions of Grape-Nuts pinged against tile and appliances and hardwood. Up rose the ugliness of Lucas's truncated nap, Bill's phone call to say he had a dinner meeting, the fact that I hadn't spoken to an adult all day, and the reality of six more hours until bedtime. "FUCK!!!" I yelled.

Predictably, cherubic fourteen-month-old Lucas looked up through the rain of cereal and happily echoed, "Fuck!"

From my third child this would have been funny. From my impressionable and perfect first, who now numbered fuck among the twenty-two words I kept thinking I should record in his baby book, this was dire.

All my life I had assumed that I would mother many children and I would love mothering them and I would mother them well. I had attended an empowering all-girls' high school that convinced an entire generation of us that the hard-driving career, the sensitive husband, the well-adjusted children . . . all of it would be ours. Some professional or academic pursuit, I was sure, would sit politely on the back burner during the years my children were small. I would revel in self-defining and immensely fulfilling maternity, as had my mother, a successful psychotherapist who put her career on hold to raise four kids. But here I stood, bored and depressed in a Grape-Nuts-strewn kitchen. I was twenty-eight. I was earning a doctoral degree, Bill was working long corporate hours, and motherhood had me blindsided.

Fuck dropped out of my vocabulary. Hearing it in my young son's mouth made the responsibility of parenting feel all the more weighty. I found myself profoundly jealous of the fact that Bill worked in an actual office in San Francisco with a room someone else filled with apples and cold cuts and bubbly water and Pop-Tarts. The commute he professed to dread sounded fabulous: a half-hour train ride during which he could sit down and read. During that first year of parenting I would be lonely for Bill all day, then seethe when he walked through the door because he hadn't been the one to battle the never-napping baby or stand for eight minutes in the supermarket checkout line with milk leaking from his breasts. I never slept for more than a few hours at a stretch and became convinced that Bill's long hours were subterfuge for the affair he was having because I had turned into such a bitch (my sage therapist mother assured me otherwise but I wasn't above some histrionic checking-of-shirt-collars-for-lipstick). I got pregnant again just after the Grape-Nuts debacle, and even though the four-child plan I had harbored since I was tiny seemed well on-track, I felt isolated from friends, distanced from my husband, and resentful about having to read esoteric eighteenth-century French plays in the sandbox while my colleagues luxuriated in libraries.

But even as the word fuck disappeared from my vocabulary, there was never a shortage of fucking in our miserable little household. I love sex. I always have. For me, sex means trust and intimacy and unparalleled physical pleasure. In the years, though, when Lucas was little and our daughter, Hannah, was born and when Xavier arrived two years later, sex became something else again. Far more crucial than any utterance of the word, the act was a desperate clinging to some semblance of a self not entirely eclipsed by maternity.

Bill and I may have been attachment parents (by force, not design), and there may have always been babies limpeted to my body or sprawled between us, but we found plenty of ways to fuck (see suggestions for Private Time in the pages ahead). We wedged intimacy into unlikely snatches of time. We did it on the closet floor when the urchins crowded us out of bed. During those dark years we discovered new positions and couples' porn and vibrators because of how desperate the happy trio—who always wanted to be held and wouldn't take bottles, who nursed constantly and ate pickily and never ever slept—were making us.

Sex was frequent, but fraught. A lonely me needed to create adult intimacy in a household subsumed by unpredictable, insatiable, nonverbal people. It was hurried or interrupted or sad. Mid-sex laughter was replaced with anxious clinging; precoital backrubs with gloomy brooding. I often cried afterward because the rest of my life felt so overwhelming.

Sex—I understood only later—was how I was maintaining the sanity other new mothers were preserving with an indulgent soak in the tub or an afternoon jog or a monthly girls' night out. In my diverse "New Moms Group" there was the occasional allusion to the toll our infants were taking on our marriages. Any mention of sex, though, amounted to how totally horrible the idea sounded. Instead of telling them that Bill and I were having plenty of (desperate) sex, I told those moms that it was reassuring to imagine—when wakened by my infant for the third time in the night—that one of them was awake as well, changing a diaper or soothing a baby around the corner. These were women who understood the immensity of the transition to maternity. They were supportive and empathetic and wise, but countless new-mothering concerns meant that sex was never a subject of real discussion.

I would have to wait five years to finally dwell on the

issues that were never aired with my New Moms. In May 2005, Xavier turned two and stopped breast-feeding. He and Lucas and Hannah all still slept in our bedroom (crazy, I know), but they had actually begun to sleep through the night. My eldest child was attending kindergarten five days a week! I got an IUD. I got a real hairstyle. Bill and I took a trip to Las Vegas that marked the beginning of what we deemed "The Renaissance." (This was my rebirth because, of course, it was I who most needed revival. Bill is an exceptionally devoted and playful father, but was never mired in the trenches as completely as I was.) Renewal meant tattooing Bill's initials into my lower back, planning a trip for two to Paris, committing myself to an occasional glass of wine with my husband, and hosting a series of erotic dance classes in my living room.

By this point—the kids being two, four, and six—we had moved across the San Francisco Bay. While I stayed in touch with the sympathetic New Moms who had seen me through those trying early years in Oakland, I had the uncommon good luck to fall in with a gang of candid elementary school mothers who were more than happy to let conversation stray from toddler sleep tactics and potty training. With somber nodding we acknowledged the way young kids taxed our marriages only to zip past this reality to compare notes on lingerie (or not), on vibrators, on the sex benefits of laser hair removal, on our favorite brands of lubricants, and how to manage sex in the afternoon with ever-more-cognizant children racing around the house.

Consciously and judiciously, at a point when my kindergartener, preschooler, and toddler were all the more vulnerable to its influence, I injected fuck right back into my parlance. Not to say that I was shouting "motherfucker!"

when someone couldn't get his car seat buckled or her
shoes tied. Bill and I weren't having sex in front of the kids
or taking up smoking or proposing orgies with their class-
mates' parents. But we made decisions such as to not censor
our favorite music just because the gorgeous chorus is "This
is fucked up, fucked up." We've gotten into the excellent
habit of feeding the little guys first then having our own
fireside dinner in the living room. I love that when the
"new me" misses the freeway exit and slips up by muttering
"shit" much to my children's narc-ish glee, I explain that
swearing is my adult prerogative, and I think they understand. I love that slipping fuck into a conversation with an
engaging kindergarten mom I'm just getting to know height-
ens some kind of intimacy and hints to this woman that
there's more to me than a classroom volunteer and lunch
packer. Most of all, I love the fact that this renaissance has
meant surpassing my old self, Bill and I having sex now
that's more interesting and frequent and satisfying than it
was *pre*kids.

As "fuck" made its way back into my life, I became more
and more fixated on the idea of sex as a central aspect of
marriage and an important, if slighted, facet of mothers'
lives. While my fellow elementary school moms and I were
discussing and evaluating and laughing about all manner of
sex stuff, I wondered if other women were having these conversations. I started asking new friends and old about masturbation and pornography and privacy strategies. From
dinner party polls and select playground conversations, I
found that nearly everyone I approached was eager to share
what I had come to think of as true tales of sex after kids (it
was Bill—leave it to my Bill—who came up with "Hump").

What *Hump* offers is a chronicle of the renaissance my

fellow moms and I have undergone. But not only that. More than a record of one community's antics, *Hump* encompasses an array of parents' experiences. In "I Touch Myself" you'll become privy to many women's views on masturbation (which dovetails nicely with the practical advice in "Secrets of the Magic Wand"). "Snip!" explores vasectomy, while "Snap!" focuses on the failure of birth control that results in inadvertent pregnancies—one met with dismay, another with joy, one eliciting elation, another abortion. In "These Are Our Bodies?! These Are Ourselves?!" you'll witness one woman's hilarious exploration of the baffling geography of the vag, while "Pleasure Party" sees a dozen women venture into the extraordinary world of sex toys. With its range of true stories, *Hump* seeks to provoke thought, to encourage conversations (or laughter, or intimacy) within marriages, and to offer a depiction of reality that will speak to myriad mothers and fathers. Most fundamentally, though, *Hump* seeks to sympathize, convince, and inspire.

Sympathize because making sex a priority in a household with children is really difficult. This is the motivation behind the "Arguments Against" chapters interspersed throughout the book. "Arguments Against" present the varied and detailed reasons—I'm sure you can come up with an easy half-dozen in about thirty seconds—why sex is not desirable or convenient or appealing while parenting young children. A few of my darkest mothering moments are writ large in *Hump*. Because this collection is not meant to suggest a facile Make-Sex-a-Priority-and-Life-Will-Be-Fabulous sort of maxim. "Back in the Saddle," "Utility Drawer," "Talk to Me, Babies" . . . practically every story in this collection illustrates the daunting realities of life with young children. Some of what follows is pretty ugly. But few parents would refute that raising children is the most challenging endeavor each of us has undertaken. While acknowledging these difficulties, *Hump* argues that making sex a priority can ease the very real struggles parents face.

Not just sympathize with these struggles but present convincing arguments that sex should be a priority because parents at the turn of the millennium are experiencing many new and conflicting pressures. We find ourselves—I'm thinking mostly of mothers here—divided on the central issue of staying-at-home versus pursuing careers. Women have been allowed revolutionary access to education and professional advancement, but we were sold a bill of goods in the experiment that sought to conjoin ambitious professionalism with dedicated mothering. Atop this central stressor, today's parents both at home and in the office are fed overwhelming amounts of contradictory and alarmist information specifying how to raise the smartest, sanest, happiest, healthiest, safest kids. Furthermore—as if maintaining a career and upholding the "cult of the child" weren't enough—mothers are suddenly also expected to wear thong-style underwear and identify with the women in *Sex and the City*. We've heard of MILF's and *Desperate Housewives* and suburban pole-dancing classes, all of which suggest that women should be professional and maternal *and* overtly sexual. This new iteration of the timeless mother-virgin-whore conundrum can amount to odd pressure, a put-upon feeling that mothers need to consider not only the latest glass-ceiling perspective and day-care repercussions, not only *Reviving Ophelia* and *Raising Cain: Protecting the Emotional Lives of Boys*, but also strip-tease courses.

The fact is that *Hump*—while conceding the difficulties

and contradictions in this—actually does encourage the strip-tease classes, or something like them (see "Kinerotics"). My suggestion is that parents should embrace this latest trend, the mother as sexual being, instead of the "cult of the child," the divisive mommy wars, and those endless overpro-grammed afternoons. *Hump* seeks to convince mothers that a good romp now and again is a healthy way to sidestep stress-ful imperatives with an act that can be self-affirming, stress reducing, and intimacy enhancing. *Hump* encourages parents to choose sex over emptying the dishwasher or watching *SportsCenter* or reading the "Seven Signs that Your Child Loves You" that babycenter.com just popped into your inbox. Be-cause a good romp now and again makes you feel good. And it makes your partner feel good. What *Hump* argues is that sex should be right there at the top of the list of ways to indulge and renew. Of course, each parent needs to choose sex on his or her own terms and in ways that are comfortable and self-inspired, but these pages suggest that more emphasis on a sat-isfying sex life needs to be a priority.

Hump seeks to sympathize and convince and *inspire* be-cause sex is important. Volatile and messy and sometimes inconvenient, yes—but honestly, how many human under-takings are so foundational? How many acts have the po-tential to feel so incredibly good? Parents are busy. Life with kids is busy. But if providing your children a model of a well-functioning marriage is one of the most important things a parent can do, and if having better and more frequent sex with your spouse will lead to a stronger marriage, then your kids won't hold it against you when you forego Candy Land for an adult foray to the bedroom (on top of the fact that most children aren't averse to the stick-the-kids-in-front-of-the-TV privacy strategy that so many parents successfully employ). With practical advice and more than a few steamy passages, this volume provides inspiration for more and better sex.

Because the sentiment undergirding each true story in *Hump* is that you really ought to toss this book aside. My hope is that a certain point in a given paragraph will move you to dogear a page or splay the collection facedown. You might grab (or purchase) a vibrator. You might view some porn (for the first time?) or sidle up to your spouse and make a dash for the bedroom. Quick!—before the toddler's up from the nap or the kids are back from school. Read on. I'll keep my fingers crossed.

PART ONE

The Hump

CHAPTER 1

Back in the Saddle

[Tips for] Easing Back into Sex:
Lubricate . . .
Medicate . . .
Inebriate.

—Arlene Eisenberg, Heidi Murkoff, and
Sandee E. Hathaway, B.S.N.
What to Expect When You're Expecting

So I've got this hunch. That if you were sitting here on the couch next to me with a cup of tea or decaf or a glass of wine, and if I asked you about your experience of labor and delivery, that you would be subject to an uncommon intensity of remembered emotion.

You might recall a crushing fear of umbilical cords twined around a small neck or the illogical anxiety that some unprecedented medical tragedy would occur during that birth, on that day, at the site of your body. You might be in the tiny minority who recalls only the serenity and pleasure she felt throughout her hypno-birth. Maybe you worried for months that you wouldn't get the epidural in time and then you did, in fact, deliver in the hospital lobby. You may have been the woman whose paralyzing fear was that of being driven literally insane by the unplumbed pain that made the women in those eerie birthing-class videos keen. Or you had been totally mortified by the mere possibility of pooping on the delivery table, then you did poop on the delivery table and pooping on the delivery table turned out to be the least of your issues. You might describe the strange details etched into your memory: the scent of the hospital's pink liquid soap, the pattern on your gown, the soothing lavender candle in the midwife's bedroomlike birth center or the packet of stale Oreos from the vending machine immediately postpartum that were maybe the most delicious thing you had ever tasted.

What if, though, I asked you about the first time you had sex after the baby?

You might guffaw or grimace or look at me blankly then quizzically, trying in vain to remember the first time you had sex after the birth of your first child.

Tales of postpartum sex are nothing, really, compared to the cathartic process of recounting labor and delivery. Which is logical. And appropriate. The birth of a child is momentous and anxiety provoking, unique and life altering, an uncommon event the average American woman experiences only twice in her life. Sex can be momentous too, of course. But sex resides on a more common and familiar plane. It follows that conversation about postpartum sex should be less healing and important, less often elicited and indulged than tales of labor and delivery. But the idea that a dreaded or frightening or glorious experience of postpartum sex shouldn't be laughed at or commiserated over or shared in appropriate and supportive ways . . . that's something I'd like to rethink.

Nathan Armstrong Holt, 8lbs., 6oz., exited his mother's uterus on April 16, 1997. His parents might have known from the way Nathan refused to turn and get his big head down into his mother's pelvis (thus necessitating a cesarean section) that little Nate might not always—as is the case with every single child—cooperate.

Nathan's nonconformism didn't start with his refusal of a "normal" delivery. One could argue that his parents might have anticipated this hitch in their birthing expectations when their son's conception occurred only six months after their first date (a very sporty but never-to-be-repeated afternoon of Rollerblading on the idyllic palm-and-oak-studded Stanford campus where Nathan's parents were conspicuous not only for their coquettish though un-coordinated efforts at blading, but also because they were significantly older—forty-five and thirty-eight—than the students thronging White Plaza). Magical Rollerblading moments led to gourmet dinner dates, which led to con-ception after Nate's mom's diaphragm mysteriously flipped, ejecting its spermicidal jelly and letting all those little swimmers past. (Nate's mom will admit in secrecy that this was probably user error, but in the company of Nate's dad, she will tell you that it was her husband's massive organ and his sexual ingenuity that accounted for the flip.) A year after his parents' courtship had begun, tiny fetus Nathan ostensibly witnessed their betrothal while in utero, fol-lowed some weeks later by much laughter on the part of his parents concerning the wedding photographer's immense care not to show the sizable six-month bump in even a single photograph in the Holts' tasteful wedding album.

Almost five weeks after the birth, Nate's mother stands in the kitchen waiting for the coffee to be ready. This coffee is her first of the day and it's almost noon. Though there is desperation in this fact, Nathan's new mother is experiencing the delicious pleasure of standing alone in a quiet kitchen, paging through a catalog while her infant sleeps.

As she looks at said catalog, her eyes alight upon a chaste camisole sort of number made of the "finest Danish green cotton." She doesn't have any idea what Danish green cotton is. She heads a public relations firm and understands that Danish green cotton is no more than a decent marketing ploy. Still, Danish cotton sounds like it might feel really good against her skin. She brings the catalog closer to her face. She holds it away. She smiles, confirming the marked similarity between the breasts under the Danish green cotton and the D-cups Nathan's mom has been unexpectedly proud of sporting since her son's birth.

Baby Nate's mom may only have known his dad for a total of thirteen months at this point, but she's familiar enough with her new husband to know that he's no lingerie man. Garters and teddies, even thong underwear (thank God, she thinks) are a turnoff for her guy. This new mom knows her husband well enough to conclude that the surest way to get him going (she doubts it'll be all that difficult given their recent new-baby sex drought) is to don one of his dress shirts with nothing on underneath.

Five diaper changes, three burp cloths, four different outfits (three for the baby, one for herself), and she's made it through the day. Right before six o'clock she hears her hus-band's car pull into the garage and Nathan's mother is pleased because she has just finished nursing the baby, who has fallen asleep next to her on the king-size bed. She has lighted candles, poured herself an unfashionably full goblet of expensive cabernet, and has her favorite Miles Davis on the stereo. She hears her man move through the mudroom into the kitchen. He calls her name but this vixen offers no reply. She waits, smiling to herself, getting—with significant relief—more and more hot about this little setup of hers.

And when the baby's father rounds the corner and gets a load of the music and the candles, the wine, and his fa-vorite white dress shirt gaping to reveal the perfect round breasts (that belong to his wife!)—when she moves forward to sit on splayed knees there on the bed—he forgets entirely that they have a child. He hurries across plush carpet and onto the bed, almost crushing his tiny son with his knee, but Nate's dad only smiles murmuring, "No harm, no foul."

Mercifully, the baby snoozes on. Mercifully because Nathan's parents like to take things slowly. Nate's mom and dad are seasoned lovers. Nathan's parents are old enough to know that maximum pleasure comes from maximum at-tention, from the right fingertips applied to the right area, from the perfect amount of pressure on the no-longer-quite-so-perfect body part.

On and on Nate sleeps and things are getting good.

Things are so good, in fact, that Ellen gives Peter the nod. A little smile and a hand on her new husband's ass mean it's okay. Of course, there is concern that childbirth will have forever altered sex. That there will be lack of sensation or serious pain (not looseness per se because Ellen has had a C-section). But none of the above! This feels good. Great, in fact. All their slow, hard work is paying off and things are heating up and this could be memorable.

When there on the bed beside his fucking parents, baby Nate explodes. He is startled from infant sleep by a fart storm. Thunderous flatulence drowns out Miles Davis and the bedsprings and drowns out his parents' laughter at such loud explosive farting from such a teeny body.

And it's a good thing Nate's folks appreciate the scatological and see real humor in this, because Nathan's dad's erection is losing traction and though Nate's dad will be able to block out the crazy farting that's going on and on and on and on beside them, though he will be able to look away from the tiny purple straining face and get his business done, Nate's mother won't be so lucky.

Which is all right. Really. Because even without an orgasm for her, this evening is a victory. This new mom actually *felt* like having sex. She herself created a situation in which she and Nate's dad had sex again! Although Ellen feels momentarily unsatisfied when Peter rolls off her, frustration is short-lived.

She reaches across the bed, away from her heavy-breathing mate. She lays a hand on the round warmth of little Nate's bald infant head. His tiny body jumps as a final belated fart thunders forth and Ellen laughs. Peter laughs too, both of them thinking that the whole experience has been just fine.

Sasha Catherine Ericson was born Thursday, February 10, 2005, to an astonishingly bright mother and a talented architect father, both of whom are unusually attractive.

Sasha's mother's driving desire from the time she was

four was to be in the Ice Capades. Because Sasha's mother is both athletically gifted and tenacious, her rarified dream came true. Sasha's mother, subsequently, was smart enough to consider maternity only after having toured the globe for a dozen years with "the show." Only after much self-reflection and adventure and many excellent years of out-spoken swearing and high heels and raucous late nights, only after marrying her hot husband and enjoying another few years of serious leisure travel did Sasha's mother one day decide that she would, in fact, like to have a baby.

This was not easy. Sasha's mother spent four years mut-tering goddammit when she felt incipient cramping or found evidence of failed conception on toilet paper or in her panties. There were two years of acupuncture, sched-uled sex, and superstitious temperature taking. Finally, Sasha's parents decided to "take a break" from the desperate business of babies and spent a month in remote outposts of the South Pacific. Post-travel nausea failed to resolve itself back in the States, was diagnosed as pregnancy, and little Sasha was born eight months later. Her intuitive mother took one look at Sasha's crooked little smile and was con-vinced that this child was the embodiment of her best friend and figure-skating superstar Patrick Reed, who had died some years before.

So it was that Sasha's mother—six weeks after giving birth—came to have the following discussion with her handsome husband over the nightly beer that was lately getting her through the evenings.

"It's all Patrick's fucking fault."

Sasha's dad looks up from the unidentifiable casserole a friend brought over. "What is?"

"That big head of his. Patrick's big fucking skull."

"He did have a big head. But what's his fault?"

"My six-week checkup this morning. I swear to you. I am not even kidding. Dr. Lu had to put three fingers up there. Not just one like before. Three fucking fingers to feel around for whatever she feels around for!" It's easier to say it like this, to swear and seem to be exaggerating. But she isn't exaggerating. Sasha's mother has developed considerable anxiety during the course of the day that her body has been forever ruined by a seven-and-a-half-pound person busting out of her vagina.

And because her husband shakes his head just the littlest bit and smiles sort of ironically, she has to say, "What."

"Just that . . . when you were having the baby, she had her whole forearm up there."

"Jesus Christ!"

"Sorry. Not helpful."

"Not helpful!"

The baby monitor bleeps and crackles, both parents looking to where it sits on the counter then away as it falls silent.

Sasha's dad takes up his wife's beer and has a long swig. "It'll be fine," he says. "I'm sure it'll be fine."

"How do you know that? My vagina's so big you could drive a fucking Volkswagen in there! What if it doesn't go back?"

"It'll go back."

"What if it doesn't?"

"Well . . ."

Sasha's attractive father leans forward and takes his beautiful wife's hand in his. Sasha's mother wants to cry because she loves this man enough to have had his child wreck her body and her sex life forever and he's going to say something incredibly reassuring and maybe this will be the night they'll have sex again for the first time even though the thought of her husband's penis anywhere near her still-recovering vagina is horrifying and from what she's heard she's completely justified in not having sex again after only six weeks.

Her dreamy husband gazes at her. "Look," he says, "if it doesn't go back . . ."

"Yeah?"

"We'll just butt-fuck."

And Sasha's mom laughs so hard that she actually pees a little. She's laughing but she's overwhelmed and soon she's weeping with gratitude and tenderness because this man is so good and so funny and Sasha's mom is thinking that even if her vagina never "goes back," at least she and her knockout husband have this.

————

When Gianna Truth Fiorucci's mother's OB visits her in the hospital, he admires the baby then wraps things up by saying he'll see her in six weeks for her postpartum. Gianna's mother then remembers reading that the six-week postpartum usually means getting a green light in the sex department. She looks quickly to her doctor. "What if," she readjusts the ice pack pressed to her crotch, "what if I make that appointment not for six weeks, but maybe like . . . sixteen?"

————

Anna Marie Grebes (an impossible-to-predict 10 lbs., 8 oz.) shocked everyone by ripping out of her mother's vagina right in the hospital lobby. Anna's petite, twenty-nine-year-old mother suffered third-degree tearing, extensive repairs of the perineum, a suture that became infected months after her doctor failed to remove it, hemorrhoids the size of large grapes, and a devastating psychological defeat when her body refused to produce enough breast milk for her cute but really large baby.

Eleven months after the birth, Anna's mother looks up from where her daughter is sitting with blocks on her best friend's living room floor. That very morning Anna's mother came to realize that the reason she had pulled her old bathrobe from the back of the closet some months ago and had taken to wearing it to and from the shower was not for warmth but to avoid the possibility of arousing her husband with her naked body (now fat and saggy and gross, she thinks, though Anna's father disagrees and would convincingly argue that he likes the way her body now seems more . . . womanly).

Anna's mom looks at her best friend and is pretty sure she's going to cry. She looks away. "Mike and I haven't done it," she says. "It's been eleven months and we still haven't had sex. I can't put a Tampax in without dying because it hurts so much." Anna's mother is now crying, which makes her feel melodramatic and defective. She's worried about the effect of no sex for almost a full year on her marriage. She's petrified at the idea of unbearable pain during intercourse. She's indescribably tired of giving blow jobs.

Mobilized, the best friend takes baby Anna for the following Saturday night. The lucky couple drives north. They check in to the sumptuous Sonoma Mission Inn, which is obscenely priced, but these are desperate times. Anna's mother loves a nice spa and Anna's father is not above desperate measures.

Drinks, dinner, a walk through a vineyard, more drinks, and Anna's parents are back in their fancy room. Astroglide and lingerie and much foreplay and more drinks and more foreplay before Anna's father is atop Anna's mother. She can feel the pressure of his penis near her vagina and she breathes. She wills herself to relax and flashes back to the gruesome horror of delivering a baby in the hospital lobby. She closes her eyes and takes another deep breath. She presses resolute hands against her husband's ass and tries to unclench her jaw as he carefully moves into her and the pain is astounding.

The pain is a burning ripping blazing that makes Diane cry out and push herself away from Mike, who is trying really hard to be patient. He lets his head fall forward so that it rests between his wife's large flaccid breasts as she begins to cry.

———

Some weeks or months after the births of Emma Jordan Sachs, Erin Leslie Dunlap, Peter Miller, and Michaela Baul, these infants' mothers were enjoying long-absent foreplay with fathers who were ecstatic to have wives who seemed ready to have sex again. Although each father was confident in his own sexual expertise, in his own preferences, and his knowledge of his wife's tastes, each dad was surprised when his wife's breasts responded to his magic touch with sudden streams of milk.

———

William Francis Ford's mother, back in the unusually frigid New England winter of 1969, went for her six-week postpartum to learn from her obstetrician not that she could resume intercourse, but that she—my Bill's sensual momma—was already pregnant again.

———————

Only eight weeks after Amanda Anne Lerner's father impregnated his wife, he indulged in an extramarital affair and left her. Six months later, the fall of 1990, Amanda's mother was teaching in the progressive Palo Alto preschool where she was surrounded by innocent and loving children, a compassionate director, and women who agreed that Amanda's father was pretty much a complete bastard. Amanda's mother—who is warm and smart and insightful—found she had her community's full and unreserved support.

By the time Amanda the fetus had softened her mother's physique with a nicely rounded belly, into the renowned preschool walked Greg. Greg was six-foot-three and had thick brown hair. Something weathered in his kind face spoke of the recent half-dozen years he had spent in Alaska. Greg happened to have a lovable three-year-old boy who was just joining Amanda's pregnant mother's morning class. Greg also happened to have a wife who had recently engaged in an extramarital affair and had left him.

Greg was living in his parents' home. Amanda's mother was living in her parents' home. Both needed companionship without the specter of long-term commitment. Both were in their late twenties; both were earthy, enlightened, and sensual. Amanda's mother was just over five feet tall and had the welcomed sense—with tall Greg as opposed to the average-height bastard husband—that she was safe and cared for by this new man. Amanda's mom shared with Greg an appreciation for the hurt and anger that are the result of infidelity, as well as a passion for the cheeseburgers at the nearby Dutch Goose.

One evening the unlikely couple pulled out of the parking lot of the Goose with a few sleeping bags mounded in the back of Greg's Volvo. On a gentle hillock near the seventh hole of the Stanford Golf Course, Shelly had the kind of ultra-sensational sex that some women experience when pregnant, but that few experience with a man who is not the father of the baby. Shelly has never enjoyed sex so much in her life. She loves this sex. Shelly doesn't exactly love Greg, but she really likes Greg and she loves having sex with him.

Amanda's mother delivers her lovely baby girl and muddles through the first six weeks of single parenting with the support of her own parents and the moms at the community-rich progressive preschool. None too soon, Amanda's overwhelmed and decidedly hormonal mother gets word at her six-week postpartum that she can indulge herself once again in Greg.

Greg, who has become, more than anything else, a close friend. At preschool pickup the following day, Amanda's mother subtly communicates to Greg that she is ready to roll. That very night he sneaks into her parents' house, into the very bedroom Amanda's mother had grown up in. Shelly is eager for companionship and affection and more of the insanely good sex she'd been having with Greg. She's dying to get a hand on his Alaskan-hewn ass and his enormous penis. She wants to rake her fingers through his thick brown hair.

What her doctor hadn't mentioned, what neither her own mother nor the preschool mothers had told her (none of whom guessed that baby Amanda's single mother needed the crucial tip about lots and lots of lubricant and taking it slow) was that there might be significant pain.

It's awful. It's horribly painful. And because Greg is a good friend but not a husband, Amanda's mother feels the need to maintain a façade of pleasure (there *is* pleasure in his chest against hers and in feeling his hard ass, just not in his enormous penis thrusting into her damaged vagina). Thank God he has to sneak back out of her parents' house pretty much as soon as they're done. Not until Greg quietly closes the door behind himself does Amanda's mother—her swollen breasts leaking, her vagina burning and aching and pulsing with the beat of her heart—creep out to the kitchen.

She is alone and worried and angry at the bastard husband. She is grateful for friendly Greg but sad too. She is weepy even though she knows she will be all right because she loves her baby girl. What seems unfair and tragic and awful is that Amanda's mother herself has to slink out to her parents' kitchen to fill a baggie with ice that she will carry back to the bedroom and press against her poor, lonely vag.

———

Lucas Francis Ford was born August 7, 1997, after two days of labor and a lot more pushing and surgery than his mother had ever thought to include in the naively optimistic "Birth Plan" she had researched and written up for esteemed Dr. Baldwin.

The evening after her calamitous experience of childbirth, Lucas's mother is trying to sleep (her nine-pound son off in the nursery) when a blond nurse leans into the room. The nurse mentions faux casually that the baby's breathing is "somewhat rapid." Lucas's mom is unable to process this information because only hours before she was so far out of her head with pain that she remembers nothing except repeatedly vomiting thin green liquid into a kidney-shaped lavender trough; then the demoralizing moment when a grandmotherly labor-and-delivery nurse pursed her lips and said, "You're just not pushing effectively." The blond nurse in the doorway, oblivious to Lucas's mom's confusion, mentions that the infant has been transferred to the Neonatal Intensive Care Unit, which doesn't sound good.

Baby Lucas will turn out to have a mysteriously contracted case of pneumonia. A large-bore I.V. will be implanted into his head for the administration of antibiotics over the course of the next seven days. The NICU nurses will try to make Lucas's frightened mother feel better when her baby wails with hunger in the unsettling silence of the NICU. "Doesn't that sound wonderful?" they'll say. "Isn't that music to your ears?" But there is no way baby Lucas's weepy mother can join in the NICU nurses' celebration of well-developed nine-pound infants' lungs, even congested, as compared to the lungs of the silent wren-size preemies surrounding her behemoth's bassinet.

Finally, Lucas's parents get to take their hearty baby home to Oakland. Now, because Lucas was born eight days after his due date then spent that shitty week in the NICU, the exhausted young family returns to their quaint bungalow just as Lucas's father's parents arrive from Massachusetts for a weeklong stay on a blow-up mattress in the living room.

Lucas's mom knows it, Lucas's dad knows it, even Lucas's grandparents know that it's stupid for Lucas's mother to insist that she feels *fine!* even though she has a fifteen-day-old baby; that she *wants* to go to the market for the makings of the caramelized pork roast that everyone will love. Call it a perverse need to impress her in-laws or her husband or herself. Call it a very basic need to get out of the house.

But it's this trip to the market—Lucas's mother still slightly hunched at the yucky twingy pain of her cesarean incisions—that shifts something in her. This is the first time she has driven the car. This is the first time she has ventured out into the world alone since having another human being emerge from her body. The yellow October afternoon seems miraculous because she is alone in rich autumn light. It turns out—she is astonished—that she is the same person she was eleven months before when not even an embryo existed and instead of gestating she was taking the bus down College Avenue to her Semiotics and Borges seminar.

Back at home she accepts not only help with the groceries but also her mother-in-law's offer to start making a salad. Lucas's mother takes her infant in her arms. She lays a hand on her husband's shoulder and gives a little jerk of her head that means he should follow her up the steep staircase to their tiny bedroom.

Once there, the baby is all but tossed onto the bed. The husband is pulled to his wife's body, her hand pressed hard to the back of his head as she kisses him. She starts unbuckling his belt and pulling at the button fly of his blue jeans.

Her hands are then on her own T-shirt, pressing the hard roundness of her newly transformed breasts. The T-shirt is up and off, the damp and crusty nursing bra flung on the floor. Her hands cup her breasts as she lies back on the bed.

Her husband slowly, quizzically pulls her hips to his. He leans down and kisses her softly on the mouth.

She kisses him harder. She pulls him to her.

Now, Baby Lucas's dad is thinking blow job at best. He's

witnessed the subtle jokes and not-so-subtle admonitions of couples who've gone before them. No sex is to be had, he's gathered, for months and months after the painful or exhausting or just plain gross birth of a baby.

But Lucas's mom has her husband's jeans off and boxer shorts down and his cock is firmly in her hand. She's accumulating saliva that she swipes on fingertips then her crotch. She's arching her hips up toward him because—much to Lucas's father's immediate arousal—she seems to want to fuck.

And there is discomfort. Lucas's young dad is unsure, actually, that this is a good idea. He doesn't thrust so much as steal his way in. And the discomfort mostly passes. Lucas's father has a sense that he might be bumping up against something vulnerable and bruised inside of her. The ceiling seems to have been lowered. He is tentative (though hard as a fucking rock) so she guides him. With her hands on his hips she shows him the new and (they hope) temporary parameters.

Kimberly is immensely relieved to be having sex. She feels cared for and renewed and astoundingly close to her husband.

And she cries. Tears run down her temples and into her ears.

Through his blinding pleasure her husband notices she's crying. He murmurs, "Aaaw."

And she laughs then in a sad burst that's really more crying than laughing and he grows still but she pulls him into her and urges him on.

She cries because going to the grocery store was stupid and now she's exhausted and fragile. It will be a horrible evening even if the caramelized pork is a triumph. She's crying because the baby is nursing all the time and not sleeping at night. The infant she wanted so badly sleeps all day, except when he's nursing. She worries when he sleeps in the day that he won't sleep at night so she wakes him from his naps; her mother-in-law says that no one ever wakes a sleeping baby and her mother-in-law is probably right.

She's crying because she has a stack of important books by her bed that she had planned to read with her infant snuggled against her chest. She has taken the book from the top of the stack a number of times. She has tried to read but there's something wrong with her brain. She can't make sense of what she reads and this terrifies her. She has the feeling that she has fallen into a dark hole. She is alone and scared and sad.

But the closeness of her husband's body, its warmth and strength and familiarity, means that just possibly he'll understand.

Slowly, slowly, he fucks her. He smoothes her unwashed hair from her forehead so he can see her eyes and she turns her face away. She loves that he is staring at her and even as she looks away she wants him to keep staring at her.

She is convinced that he understands because he is here fucking her and no one else on the planet fucks her. This is special fucking because no one would think they'd be up here doing it with a fifteen-day-old baby. This is secret fucking with her in-laws right below them in the kitchen. She's the only one who gets to fuck him and he's the only one who gets to fuck her and this might prove that she is the same person she was before the baby hurt her body and addled her brain. She just happens to have fallen into a dark hole and she needs help finding a way out.

CHAPTER 2

Kinderotics

If men today appear to be more interested in all manner of sexual stimuli than women are, if they are the major consumers of pornography and prostitution, and if they say in surveys they'd like to dabble around with as many gals as will approach them on the street with a clipboard in hand, we gals can only reply, It's a man's world, designed for the pleasures of men; and on those rare occasions when a female-friendly sexual nerve is tapped, females respond with crows and roars of hunger and delight.

—Natalie Angier,
Woman: An Intimate Geography

I move through never-ending witching hours when Bill is thousands of miles away and being in the house with three small children is too much. I gather them together and we take to the street. What I need is for this night to differ—in any small way—from the hundreds I have spent serving my children's desires at the expense of my own.

Front doors are closed, though. Front yards are empty.

The promise of a calming, satisfying, time-killing walk— of a witty exchange with a neighbor! of commiseration with another mother out walking with her children!—fails to materialize. One-year-old Xavier refuses stay in the stroller, the dog pulls tirelessly at the leash, Hannah and Lucas insist on picking the flowers that I have explicitly told them not to pick.

It is this very evening when the old woman in the broad-brimmed hat suddenly appears on the sidewalk before us. She beams. "Savor these days," she says to me. "These are the best days of your life." I swear her eyes well with tears. "It goes by so fast."

That very morning I had experienced a blissful moment of wonder and beauty and patience when my three children awoke to find that one of the seeds in the cups on the kitchen sill had pushed up through its dark soil. Come five o'clock, though, I am devoid of wonder and beauty and patience. I want to tell the old woman so. I want to tell her that by five o'clock I am tired and anxious and achingly bored. I want to explain how terrified I feel (almost always late at night) when I sense that entire weeks are indeed rushing by. I want to share how uneasy I feel when I find myself wishing time away. Mostly, though, I want to smack the well-meaning crone because never have evenings crept so slowly.

———

But finally, Lucas is in kindergarten.

Monday afternoon pickup. On the after-school agenda is the local library's story hour for toddlers, then Mommy and Me Ice-Skating, then Trader Joe's, and I am acutely aware that the eight minutes here with these moms constitute the highlight of my day. I move a little closer to Allison, who has angled her double stroller toward mine in the vain hope that our children might occupy themselves and not dash off like Ruby's toddler, who has made a break for the blacktop. Seven minutes and I will be sucked again into the vortex that is my children. With Xavier out of the stroller and onto my hip, with three-year-old Hannah sitting on my feet with an arm wrapped around each of my calves, with six minutes remaining, I lean close to Allison, who looks a little beleaguered, and say, "I have the best idea."

"Anything," she sighs.

"Seriously. This is what we need." I call Ruby over. Ruby will definitely do this. "Ruby!" I yell.

She looks from the errant daughter she is halfheartedly chasing. She scoops her up and jogs back to us.

"Kim has an idea," says Allison.

"Thank God," says Ruby, whose dark hair is newly shorter. Its scarlet "color wash" provides sultry evidence of how Ruby is forever trying to inject excitement into suburbia. "We need an idea," she says as she shifts her daughter to the other hip.

"Anything," says Allison. "I'll do anything."

I pause. "Catherine Rose."

"Babysitter?" Allison brightens. Allison could not possibly appear more different from Ruby, what with the nononsense short haircut she's had for a decade, her locks left their natural salt-and-pepper because Allison "would rather nap than go to the beauty parlor."

I shake my head. "Not a babysitter."

"Massage therapist?" says Ruby, now that guessing is a game. "Prescribing psychiatrist?"

"Nope," I say. "Erotic dancer."

"Erotic dancer?" Allison's afternoon lineup includes a stop by Weight Watchers, where she will be dismayed at how tenaciously the baby pounds are clinging. "We need an erotic dancer?"

"*Ooooh!*" this from Ruby. "We do! We *do* need an erotic dancer!"

Three Saturdays later and we've corralled Ellen and Liz and Simone, Whitney, Katherine, Tess, and Karen.

And here in my living room, impossibly and unpredictably and even before Catherine Rose has made the scene, this evening feels even better.

———

Better than six months before with my younger sister, Ellis, the bride-to-be. My progressive sister who had been dying to take erotic dance lessons. My sister who had just spent the afternoon leading her group of accomplished and gorgeous twenty-something bachelorettes in a bonding sort of art project that involved painting on our naked breasts (my tiny, saggy boobs were used as the demo; my post-lactation breasts were bared first because my sister was sure that they would be the perfect thing to make her pert and shapely twenty-six-year-old peers feel more comfortable about stripping down and painting up). We went around to different stations set up in the high-ceilinged and window-seated North Beach apartment, pressing squares of pretty colored paper to wet, painted flesh. The resulting flowers and stars and swirls would be made into a collage, or a series of wishes for my sister's marriage, or the thank-you notes that one among our numbers would send to her unsuspecting mother-in-law.

The craft project was conceived as a mere warm-up by Ellis, who has worked at the Berkeley Free Clinic and Planned Parenthood and is unafraid to announce her "pro-sex" stance in any social context. My sister has teal and blue and purple extensions in her black hair and chickens in her backyard in Oakland. It was Ellis who would soon convince me that Brazilian waxing has far less to do with bikini line than sensation. A pioneer in laser pubic-hair removal and an attendee of Good Vibrations' Erogenous Zones Workshops, she decided to get married last summer at an early twenty-six—the first in this group of nubile lovelies—because she was so passionately in love.

Soon after our breasts were once again clothed and the evening's first round of mojitos had been mixed, Catherine Rose was suddenly in our midst. Twenty-somethings leaned closer to each other. "Is that her?" They looked up from their cocktails. They sat taller on the Chelsea couch in their Citizens of Humanity jeans and giggled. "That must be her. It's *her*."

Catherine Rose wore sweats, a long black coat, gray Converse sneakers. Her hair was mousy and mid-length with little discernable style, a pretty nimbus around her heart-shaped face. Gold-rimmed spectacles distracted from eyes that were deep brown, big, and shimmery. Catherine Rose gazed out at the beauties and smiled. Warm and unassuming, she said, "Hi."

Though even here—even among the comely bodies of my sister and her friends with their effortless lissome grace, their prenatal hips, breasts not stretched and warped and sucked and bitten and tugged, whose sleepless nights were elected and full of vodka and Red Bull and hot guys—even in their firm bodies there was hesitation—the rounding of shoulders, a cautious self-preserving look in young eyes. This hesitation? It was the power of sex, the power of the female body. I understood then that these women were young. These women had boyfriends. They hadn't given birth or cleaned up multiple children's vomit from the crevices in the backseat of the car. These women hadn't soothed night terrors or witnessed a nursery-schooler's first knock-knock joke. These women were, in fact, girls.

From the inebriated North Beach hostess, Catherine Rose accepted a plate heaped with premarinated chicken and minute rice and salad with lite dressing. Catherine Rose hoovered her meal, smiling all the while in an amused and tranquil way. She looked slowly, peacefully from one to another of the lovelies. She nodded softly as she chewed and listened, content as these young ladies lauded the mojitos Catherine Rose just had to try (she did), spoke of how great the weekend had been so far (it had), shared their boob prints and tales of the Sutro Baths spa, and chatted about how exciting it was that Catherine Rose had finally arrived.

She then inquired about a bathroom. She smiled a feline smile and made a coy yet serene allusion to slipping into something more comfortable. Time collapsed and before we had sipped at our next round of drinks, she was back. There was no way the sequined black catsuit and slutty four-inch platforms were more comfortable than the sweats, but Catherine Rose was transformed.

In my living room that warm October evening half a year later, there occurs the same transformation. Catherine Rose has shown up at the stroke of eight. Tonight she is with her striking tattooed assistant, Daphne, and has opted for loose jeans instead of sweats. The puffy mousy hair and the gold-rimmed spectacles I have promised this group of middle-age mothers, though, are delivered.

Again Catherine Rose accepts a heaping plate, only this time it's filet mignon, Gruyère polenta, mâche salad, and clafoutis with pear. Instead of a mojito, she receives a Dorothy Parker from Ruby, whose dark bangs are pulled to the side with a small clip, two playful pigtails sticking out in back. Catherine takes a long savoring sip, then another. She smiles and Ruby is won over by this mousy woman who not only loves this drink—a delicious mix of Champagne, vodka, lemon juice, and some secret ingredient Ruby refuses to divulge—but who also listens attentively to Ruby's animated discourse on the fabulously cynical and iconoclastic writing of the drink's namesake.

As she had in the North Beach apartment, Catherine Rose wolfs her meal then excuses herself to the powder room. While she transforms, Daphne rolls out yards of purple faux fur in the living room we have cleared of furniture. It's salt-and-pepper Allison who grows curious enough to amble over and ask, "What's all the fuzzy fabric for?" Daphne gives a sexy pout. "You don't want rug burns. The two-hour class is all about floor work." While we mothers mentally replace more familiar ideas of sit-ups and leg-lift "floor work" with writhing sexy crawling, Catherine Rose emerges.

Not a catsuit this time. For suburban mothers clad in yoga pants and T-shirts, Catherine Rose has donned a beautifully beaded aqua G-string—not so much as a thong—with a similarly beaded and fringed bikini top covering her small breasts. On exaggerated metallic stilettos she glides toward the gaggle of us. Simone falls silent. Ruby grabs my elbow and utters, "Whoa."

The Dorothy Parkers give way to the expensive red wine Whitney brought from her husband's cellar and instead of recent college grads, we number the founder of a major law firm, a woman who heads a department at Stanford, two M.D.'s, and a VP of a major local software company. But that's not why tonight feels different. And it's not entirely about the bodies, either, though part of the difference lies there.

These hips are wide and soft—thirty-four-, thirty-nine-, forty-four-year-old hips. Hips made more ample by the passage of a child or two or three. Breasts and bellies are loose and silvery stretch marked. Even the one of us who is an adoptive mother has gravity-tolled breasts that would sag practically to her navel if it weren't for a good bra. With our thick thighs, with our dimples and our stress incontinence, Simone, Ruby, Liz, Ellen, Whitney, Tess, Allison, and Karen, all of us have gamely formed the circle because we, more so than the nubile lovelies, are the ones who need this.

Catherine Rose comes to the center. She graces us with her beatific smile and her tranquility. With a nod of her head in Assistant Daphne's direction, there is music. Just for us Catherine Rose has arranged a playlist entitled "Moms." It's too good: a rap remix of Split Enz's "I Got You" is followed by Depeche Mode then Missing Persons' "What Are Words For?" in some club-type nouveau form and we sing along because we loved these songs in the ninth grade, and so did Catherine Rose, who further wins us over by revealing that she's thirty-seven. But this music is not simple nostalgia. These iterations are hip and edgy and salt-and-pepper Allison leaves off singing, "There's no use talking at all—" to cry, "this song never used to sound this good."

Swaying, taking languid steps in her strappy high heels, Catherine Rose begins to move. She turns, looking to each one of us, her eye contact coy but so desirous you'd swear she wants you. Ruby calls out, "God, this is such a turn-on!" as our bodies—tall skinny Simone, curvy Allison, each of us blotchy or slack or full-figured—begin to move with her.

"Ladies." In Catherine Rose's sultry tone it's a mantra. "Ladies. There are two secrets."

I know them from my sister's weekend and it's all I can do to not shout out the answers. I contain myself while she continues to tantalize with sexy hip-swaying movement. She swivels to be sure that none of these moms knows the answer then raises a single brow as if to impart the most illicit of information. "Posture," she says, though no one thinks of Emily Post. "Posture, ladies. And pacing."

"Now," she calls out with another swivel and each of us feels entirely included and ready to do whatever she suggests. "It's time to find"—she looks from Simone to Katherine—"our inner Nadias."

"As in," laughs Ruby, "Comaneci?"

Catherine Rose turns in the center of the circle, smiles serenely and says, "Exactly."

"Arms up!" Her graceful arms lift overhead, her knees angled slightly toward each other. "Forget everything your yoga teacher told you and *really arch* the low spine." Catherine Rose does so and she's stunning. "Breasts forward, ladies, shoulders back. *Stick* that landing! Now . . . drop your arms . . . to your sides."

Backs arch, asses protrude, breasts jut. Outsized overaged gymnasts drop arms to their sides and we are suddenly a roomful of the wanton.

It's then that the reality strikes. This transformation is only possible because not a single toddler's hand is pulling on any of ours. No children are wailing that they need us to read a story, that they spilled their juice, that "someone needs to wipe my bummy!" It is past our children's bedtimes. We mothers are awake and together and it's nine o'clock! Our husbands are home with our kids and this alone is glorious. No baby is crying. No one is nursing or whining or even being sweet.

"Now bend a knee," suggests Catherine Rose, "just a bit." The bent knee makes a significant difference for Ruby and tall Simone, and Catherine Rose exudes approval. "Ladies!" It's a breathy whispery sound. "You are *slinky*."

And these are no longer mothers' bodies. We find divinely racy confidence in pulled-back shoulders. We slow the pace, as Catherine Rose instructs, to half as fast as the beat.

Slowly our hips dip and thrust. Left then right, slowly. Because this is another tenet, one not to be forgotten: "The hips"—here Catherine Rose raises an admonishing finger as though this were more crucial even than finding our inner Nadias—"the hips never, ever stop moving."

And they don't. We sway. We bend knees and breathe. We do the "Head Flip" with imaginary hip-length blond hair. We mothers gyrate. Allison gives the "Figure-Eight" a go. Ruby executes a couple of serious "Thrusts." Then Catherine Rose asks us to seek out a partner, and tall, buxom Simone, who sits coyly at my sexy feet giving me feedback on my "Nasty" says, "This is *so* fun."

"Now, ladies." Catherine Rose wants each of us to find space against walls that Assistant Daphne has denuded of their art. "You might want," again, breathy, and we are so eager to hear the sensual wisdom from that bow of a mouth that we aren't even disappointed when she says, "to remove rings and watches to avoid scraping the paint." Wedding bands, watches, guard rings given in honor of children's births . . . all of them are shed. We mothers recognize the symbolism and we are liberated.

"Here is the rule for this exercise." Catherine Rose smiles a suggestive smile. She moves to the wall, places a languid palm against it. "You need to keep contact with the wall at all times. With at least one body part. With any body part."

Daphne has put on some edgy remix of "Sexual Healing," which is slow, but Catherine Rose's gyrating hips are slower.

"The wall . . ." Our professional stripper guru (for our Catherine Rose was "in the business" for nine years) speaks in a voice that mesmerizes. "The wall is the best lover you've ever had. The wall is to be trusted." She tells you to begin and with your fingertips or your hip or your knee touching the wall, you smile at the ribald wisdom in her voice. You love the ironic metaphor she's creating because it reveals that your sex mentor is not only alluring, but smart too. "The wall," Catherine Rose builds to her finish, "is silent and strong and the wall is *there for you*."

We are then to close our eyes. "So you can really enter your body," she tells us. "So you can really *feel* what's happening inside of you. So you can sense what kinds of transformations are taking place." Though I, of course, can't resist. I peek. I look over only to find Catherine Rose making out with gorgeous Daphne on the purple faux fur, which is incredibly juicy, a nugget I can't wait to share with my "ladies."

Marvin Gaye leads to a hip remake of Berlin's "The Metro" and Catherine Rose asks us to form two lines facing each other. We are to make eye contact with each other and this—gauging from bursts of nervous laughter, from the way hips halt and hands come up to mouths or reach for glasses of booze—is a challenge. We mothers have been transformed, but the fact remains that we know each other in the context of elementary school hallways and playdate pickups. One among us has recently suffered a radical hysterectomy, another just lost identical twin girls at twenty weeks' gestation. Our bodies exist in the reality of mundane pleasures and struggles, in the experience of boredom and stress and loss. Compound this with cultural resistance to open sensuality and eye contact during an erotic dance class proves difficult. But Whitney laughs because it's really fine to acknowledge how ridiculous this all seems and Simone calls out "Ellen!" as though alarmed, but then reassures her with, "It's just, I swear, you look so good!" So it's here—in the eye contact, in the way Catherine Rose insists we "keep working, ladies" in the always-swaying hips and the big-toe-dragging-turn-a-little-to-each-side sexy walk—that intimacy blooms.

Catherine Rose looks out over us and smiles her languorous smile. Over the course of the last fleeting hour she teaches us "Butt Show" and "Stairmaster" and "Peep." Her body has known no series of infants soiling and distorting ("I love to sleep far too much to have kids," she had said while finishing her clafoutis, those of us within earshot thinking this sounded infinitely wise), but Catherine Rose draws something important from each of us. She is middle-aged like we are. She has mousy brown hair and she's flat-chested and we adore what she unleashes.

We make good use of the fuzzy fabric, willowy and buxom Simone startling us all when she lowers her statuesque body onto all fours, her height belying the flexibility that allows her to look every inch the stripper—back arched, knees apart—while stalking toward Liz. Allison, though, crawling across the fur opposite Simone, bursts into head-hanging laughter when she realizes that she looks more like a diaper-bottomed baby than a show girl.

Then Allison seems downright inept as she grinds into Katherine's lap in the wing-backed chair we have pulled into the middle of the room for the lap dance segment. But—astonishing!—Allison gives Katherine's wandering hand this coquettish slap (the slap nowhere in Catherine Rose's repertoire thus far). Allison suddenly seems like some kind of professional. As if all the earlier ineptitude was some sort of tease. "My God, Allison," cries Ruby, "you were made for this!"

Back in the loose standing circle, Simone leans close to me and declares Catherine Rose "the sexiest thing I have ever seen." I consider this because it seems true, but just then Ellen executes a spectacular Butt Show. It's real and sassy and heartfelt, and she turns on her non-stilettoed heel to *"take it away"* from Ruby who must be wanting more, and I suggest to Simone, "Ellen just might be sexier!" My arm moves around Simone's shoulder and we laugh, boundaries fluid, bedtimes and pacifiers and loveys forgotten. Thick-thighed and pudgy-tummied, Simone and I watch, wondering if maybe our sweet Ellen just might be some kind of secret sexpot.

Finally the circle of maternal bodies loses its shape as we crowd into the foyer. We wave, Ruby calling, "We need more strip tease next month!" as Catherine Rose and Daphne disappear into the pitch of the warm suburban night.

Dressed not in beaded aqua G-strings but in sweatshirts and flip-flops, we mothers trickle, in pairs and trios, out the front door. We've taken up forgotten glasses of wine, bottles of water, steaming mugs of the decaf Whitney was thoughtful enough to make. We head out onto the porch. Ellen and Simone squeeze into the big chair, Ruby and Allison and I on the settee, Liz sitting criss-cross-applesauce on the porch planks. There are expectant, hopeful husbands at home, but men—it turns out—are not the point of this evening. Each of us will have kindergarteners and toddlers and fussy infants to placate in the morning, but only now do they begin to creep in on the periphery. Together, our inner Nadias commune. Each of our lower backs are slightly arched, our shoulders held back. Something of the slow pacing informs the cadence of our voices, and our minds move half as fast as the beat of the music drifting through the open front door. We sit on the porch, we sexy mommas, and let it get late.

CHAPTER 3

Utility Drawer

S o," he says.

And I laugh. My mother's colleague—an esteemed local psychiatrist—sits on his big squashy couch across from the smaller squashy armchair I've chosen.

"So." I say it this time and laugh some more. This laughter feels good, honest, and real. I'm sure that my mom, who has consulted with this man as a colleague a couple of times a week for almost a decade, has told Tom all he needs to know about why I've come. Tom, who has short gray hair and a distinguished gray beard, is a big man, handsome, a perfect cross between Hemingway and my gentle, wise theory professor. He feels, finally sitting before me in person, something like an old friend my mother talks with a lot but who happens to live across the country, or a favorite cousin of hers I've never met. I like and trust him by association. And because I'm desperate.

"I'm probably," I say, "supposed to talk about why I'm here."

"Sure."

I tuck a foot under me, settle in. Fifty minutes stretch before me—without my two, four, or six-year-old tugging at my sleeve, no dishwasher to unload, no stray shoes to search for everywhere then fish from beneath the couch— nearly an hour of self-indulgent introspection.

"The thing is," I begin, "most everything is really good. The kids are getting manageable—well, mostly—and the writing's going well. Bill has a new job in finance that he really likes, and even though he's traveling a lot, things with him are great. We've been to Las Vegas twice in the last six months. Just the two of us."

"That does sound good." Tom smiles.

"Yeah. So after all those years of being pregnant or nursing I feel like I've got my life back. More fun, a lot less dark."

"And that feels good."

"So good. It's crazy. But then . . ."

The corners of Tom's mouth turn down. I furrow my brow.

"Sometimes. Not all that often. God, who am I kidding. It's pretty much every night. Mostly when Bill travels, but even sometimes when he's home." My voice holds steady only because I am here with Tom, not in the infuriating, desperate midst of it.

"I'll be going through all these little bedtime routines that are supposed to be so great for kids and I start feeling this dread. All three have been such godawful sleepers. I'll be reading a story or singing some crap song or kissing a zillion stuffed animals good night and all I can think about is how none of us will be asleep for hours and how if I were a tougher parent who actually had some kind of backbone I could be out in the other room watching *Six Feet Under*."

"Mmmm." Tom nods.

"It'll be nine o'clock and they're wide awake and I'm getting more and more pissed off because I shouldn't have to lie in my kids' beds, with them manipulating the crap out of me."

Tom leans forward, bridging some space between us.

"But still, I cave. It's awful. I end up lying there almost every single night in a little twin bed with both Hannah and Xavier. It's hot and totally uncomfortable but I lie there super-still, seething, just hoping to God they'll fall asleep. And of course they don't. Xavier's plastered to my front. Hannah's mashed up against my back, doing this thing where she fiddles with my earring, whining that playing with my earring is the only way she'll ever be able to fall asleep."

There in Tom's office I'm shuttled back to the night before. In the dark heat of tangled blankets my daughter's hot face is impossibly close, my son's body pressed against mine. Because I have threatened to revoke a privilege if Hannah touches my ear one more time, she is now sitting up little by little with this crafty grin that makes itself felt even in the dark. Upright, she refuses to lie back down. I remind her that I have the power to revoke a privilege. I start to say that I will cancel the next day's playdate, but that would mean a long afternoon with a surly child. In ominous tones I tell her that I will move out of the bed where she wants me and onto the bedside chair where I want to be. She lies flat.

But then her little feet start up. They slide forward. Knobby kid toes tap against my shins even as I move my legs as far away as I can without pushing my son out of the bed. I lie rigid and outraged between my younger children. Again, I threaten to move to the chair. The feet still. Just in time for Xavier to wrap his sweaty arms around me and for Hannah to insist that the comforter be held right up to our chins.

I remind myself that I am the adult (Bill is in New York) and that I shouldn't allow such controlling behavior. I am also, though, desperate for sleep. Desperate for sleep, and also a little afraid. We've been past this point. There have been nights (Bill was in Chicago or Stockholm or Atlanta) when I've totally lost my shit. I've screamed and yelled and pushed and pulled. I've locked my daughter in her bedroom and I've locked myself in mine and nothing has helped.

So I lie there.

And they lie there.

Hannah whines, "If you don't hold the comforter just like this, I'll never *ever* fall asleep." Then, in this slow kind of sing-songy voice that makes me feel like I'm being held underwater, she goes, "Mom-my . . . I'm not ti-red . . ."

I want to love her bright strength, her persistence, her incredible force of will, but her needling lilt infuriates. I lurch upward. I swivel toward her and she cringes, which appalls me. I pull Xavier to my sweating front because the poor toddler is honestly scared of what his mother might unleash next. I suppress the screaming that threatens my every fiber. I jangle, I smolder. I want to grip my daughter's perfect shoulders and shake her. I have suddenly become unhinged enough—again this night—that I will not be able to fall asleep for hours. Even if they both nodded off this very moment I would be stuck in the roiling, amped-up nastiness of it. It will be midnight before I am asleep. The whole next day will be horrific and I cannot stand it.

I rip off the covers and stalk out of the room with Xavier on my hip. I slam my daughter's door. I hear her scrambling out of bed and across the hardwood. She throws herself at the door that I have been advised by my trusted pediatrician not to lock but whose knob I pull with my free hand—ever the bad parent—to hold it shut.

And some nights I do scream. I get close to her face in her narrow little bed and I scream: "What am I supposed to do with you!?"

I scream so loudly that my throat burns and Xavier cries and then I cry because this is not how I want to parent. I don't want to be a person who shoves her children's hands away from her body. I don't want to threaten and scream and grab my kids' shoulders so tightly that I have to check for bruises the next day.

Bedtime goes on and on. Time-outs double and treble. I cave and cave further and let Hannah into my bed where she insists on more earring fiddling and I can't take it. I tell her in my kind but firm voice that this behavior is not okay. I mutter in my angriest voice that she is being a jerk and a brat. I yell that she will have to get out of my bed and go to sleep in her own room . . . alone! even though I know that it is unconscionable to frame sleeping in her own room alone as the ultimate punishment.

Still—perhaps genuinely untired, perhaps genuinely afraid of falling asleep only to face the nightmares she's been having (no small wonder)—Hannah needles and whines and kicks and fiddles and twists. I grab Xavier and charge out of my own room, my daughter fast on my heels. With one hand I drag her to her room. I throw her in and scream for good measure.

On the floor just outside her door I sit with Xavier falling asleep in my arms. Six-year-old Lucas comes to his doorway and gazes at me, just to be sure everything's all right.

It gets to be ten, it approaches eleven, and still Hannah maintains her monologue from the bed I have forced her to lie in under threat of more harm. Even so, she sneaks to her forbidden doorway. She sings her needling "Mom-my . . . I'm not ti-red" and I want to thrash upwards. I want to slam out the front door and never come back.

At eleven all possibility of getting up early the next morning to read my book alone with a cup of coffee has evaporated. Together she and I have dashed all hope because it's then midnight and I am raging and smoldering and muttering, "This is a fucking nightmare."

Again, Xavier cries and I cry. And the nights when I have yanked and tugged and screamed, Hannah cries too.

So my psychotherapist mother suggests maybe I want to go see her colleague. Maybe about some medication. Our family's proclivity toward depression, anxiety, and substance abuse, coupled with her solid faith in the efficacy of selective serotonin reuptake inhibitors, lead her to believe I might benefit from a quick visit.

"Psychopharmacology is amazing stuff," I agree over a cup of tea in the house I grew up in a few miles from ours and where I purportedly didn't sleep through the night until I was five. "But I'm not anxious," I tell her, "or depressed," which my mother, my closest confidante, believes.

In the eye of a bedtime maelstrom a few nights later,

though, I sit rigid in the hallway outside Hannah's room. Xavier has nodded off in my blazing arms, Hannah is banging only desultorily against the door I guard.

With the telephone to my ear, I am teary and exhausted. I say to my mom, "Maybe I do need to go see Tom." And though I can't see the expression on her wise and empathetic face, the way she says, "Good," makes me pretty sure the two of them have already cooked up a plan.

"Bedtime sounds," he says, there on his squashy couch, "really hard."

"Yeah. It's awful."

"So," he says.

I chuckle at how this little word we started with is a sort of refrain, underscoring how these fifty minutes have already rendered the horror of bedtime distant, laughable.

"I have some thoughts." Tom's elbows settle on his knees. "First, it doesn't sound like you're depressed. You sound really good."

I nod.

"It just seems like you could use a little . . . patience."

"Yes."

"Here's what I'm thinking. Although you're not depressed, one option would be to take a very low dose of any number of antidepressants. Prozac is the obvious one. More and more frequently a very small dose—five milligrams, a quarter of the usual recommendation—is being prescribed to buy people . . . a little patience. I wouldn't expect you to notice any changes, just that when you lie there feeling trapped and when you're afraid of . . . losing control . . ." he waits for me to acknowledge that this isn't overstatement.

I nod.

"We might . . . take that edge off."

I smile. "Sounds good."

"Now, there are some side effects."

"Sure." This isn't worrisome. This is the voice-over at the end of the allergy medication commercials, the list he's mandated by law to deliver.

"Nothing serious and only reported in a small percentage of the population. With such a small dose I'd be surprised to see anything. There's loss of appetite, lethargy, drowsiness . . ."

All fine.

". . . sexual dysfunction . . ."

Less fine. I shift in my comfy armchair and observant Tom slows.

"Out of curiosity," I say, "what does sexual dysfunction actually mean?"

I will not, under any circumstances, give up the solace of sex. I see myself leaving my children's lurid rooms once they have finally fallen asleep, my own self still jangling. In those moments it's Bill's body I want. When he isn't traveling, when I get to crawl in next to him, his male presence lessens the horror I've abetted. Lying beside him I'm no longer a (terrible) mother. His body in the night—however illogically—is what convinces me that I'm not doomed to churn in mother-child ugliness forever.

"Our sex life," I say to Tom, "is kind of important to me."

"Sure. Well, there's the obvious dysfunction: decrease in desire. Mostly that. But it can also manifest in the prolonged sense that you are about to have an orgasm, but that it's difficult to achieve. Or you don't have one at all."

"Yikes."

"Again," he reassured, "side effects are highly unlikely at this dose."

Miraculous is none too strong a word. It was exactly as Tom promised. Nothing changed except that bedtime rolled around and I would lie between little bodies that were pudgy and good-baby-smelling instead of oppressive and sour. The earring fiddling wasn't annoying and my kids made me feel cozy instead of trapped. Hannah would ask some convoluted question in her ongoing and previously ultra-disturbing obsession with death. "If you're on a motorcycle," she would begin, "and you're on the way to the market but you get killed, do you ever get to the market?" To which I would reel off some fanciful answer about not getting to the market per se, but probably going right straight up to heaven where they have better, bigger candy-filled markets (my firmly agnostic self having no problem post-Prozac with this type of built-to-reassure illusion). Xavier would have already fallen asleep cuddled against me, and—because I was not smoldering with repressed hostility, because I was not ready to unleash who-knew-what, because I was a woman who had figured out one small way to take care of herself—Hannah too would drift right off.

Bedtime improved radically, but bedtime still meant Bill falling asleep midstory in Lucas's room or Xavier's. It meant a small body or two sprawled in the matrimonial bed. Bedtime never meant sex.

At a convenient three p.m. on a Saturday a few weeks after my watershed appointment with Tom, Bill has set Lucas up at the computer, Hannah and Xavier in front of *Dora the*

Explorer. He sprints upstairs and locks the door to the bedroom, where I await, having extracted the vibrator from the depths of the sock drawer. The silver bomber has become a necessity given that Bill and I have an average of twelve minutes before Hannah (always Hannah) gathers that something interesting might be going on in our unusually quiet household.

Eight minutes go by, then ten, and even with the trusty bomber, it's not looking good for me.

At my urging Bill does his thing just as the pounding begins on the door, four-year-old Hannah yelling, "Open up! I can break this down, you know!"

With a sympathetic kiss, Bill leaves me to my devices.

When I descend fifteen minutes later he looks up from where he's helping with a gigantic floor puzzle of puppies and kittens all mounded together. "Did you get it done?"

"Yeah," I say. "But touch and go." Then, with a little concern in my voice, "I wonder if this is the dysfunction."

After another couple of romps and a silver-bombing mission of my own while Bill is in London, we decide with a reassuring minimum of distress that my newfound "patience" seems to be exacting its toll. The Prozac seems to be acting just as Tom warned it might.

A few evenings later Bill is busy arranging the kids in some postprandial art project when he half-teases, "Go on up and get a head start. You know . . . the dysfunction and all."

At Blockbuster that weekend I hold up *Home Alone 3* and call out to him, "Maybe we should get this for the guys . . . on account of the dysfunction."

Driving back from the zoo Bill says, "I'd be willing, if you really want, to work on the dysfunction when we get home."

In the bedroom we slow things down, we speed things

up. We try different positions, more and less lubricant, long-forgotten tricks, and a few new ones. Nothing helps much. Mostly I do get off, but it's like some kind of ass-kicking workout where you're ultimately satisfied but the process is so taxing you wonder if it's worth it.

When I sketch the situation in broad terms for my mom she says, "That's surprising." She gets her professional far-away look, the one that means she's generating a diagnosis or a solution. "That kind of reaction is really surprising with such a small dose. But I'd wait and see. Most side effects go away after a few months."

I talk to my pro-sex nurse-practitioner sister, Ellis. "That is so weird," she says. "Five milligrams? Weird." Then, because she's almost a decade younger than I am and doesn't have kids yet, or hasn't thought through the absurdity of our fifty-three-year-old babysitter in the play-room while Bill and I fuck upstairs, she says, "Maybe get Marta to come over so you can really take your time."

The following Sunday morning Bill and I are only a few minutes into it but very little is happening and I'm tired of the whole thing.

When it hits me.

"Wait a second," I say to Bill. I zip downstairs naked, not a single head turning from the elaborate fort that Bill's pay-ing each kid a quarter to build. I stand before the "utility drawer."

Now, even I understand that the amount of pride I take in my utility drawer is a bit odd. In my grandmother's house, as in Ellis's, this would be the "messy drawer." In most others it's the "junk drawer." It was referred to as such in our first tiny house in Oakland. But the drawer I pull open in my search is no messy junk drawer. I myself transformed this drawer with excellent organizers that separate the Scotch and packing and masking tapes from the various screwdrivers from the spare keys from the battery-powered emergency radio from the extra fuses. When I pulled open the utility drawer for Bill on the evening of its organization, he asked if my mania was maybe a desperate and "kind of sad" attempt to gain control over a life that was essentially out of control. Bill had articulated an important truth and I gracefully accepted it. His insight did nothing, though, to pale my contentment. Granted, enough stuff gets stashed in there that most days I can't actually see the organizers, but the point is, they're there.

The point is, I know the exact location of what I lack, there in the farthest section in the rear of the utility drawer.

Back upstairs I straddle Bill, grinning, one hand behind my back, the silver bomber aloft in the other.

"Say good-bye," I whip out two C-size batteries, "to what was never dysfunction. That was a sad pair of overused batteries!"

Deftly I change them, the bomber's renewed verve delicious in my grip. I lean forward and kiss Bill.

I tell him, "Nine minutes left."

To which he says, "Have at it."

CHAPTER 4

Arguments Against

As early as 1957, a landmark study by E. E. LeMasters claimed
that an astounding 83 percent of new parents went through moder-
ate to severe crisis in the transition to parenthood.

—John M. Gottman, Ph.D., and
Susan Schwartz Gottman, Ph.D.,
And Baby Makes Three

B ut oh my God. There are still these evenings. Even
now that all three kids (mostly) sleep through the
night. Even when they can entertain themselves and are capable of packing their own lunches when threatened.

There are the nights that follow the afternoons of elementary school pickup where you have to park a mile away
then carry your littlest, who is four and who is not so little
anymore, and who weighs half what you do, which means
the schlepping can just about suck the soul right out of
you. You do soccer drop-off, playdate drop-off, Starbucks
because you feel like you really need a little something even
though a better mother would clearly take the four-year-old
to the park. Then, of course, the little one drops his full
kid's cocoa right onto the floor (uncomprehending childless

people in line giving you the stink-eye) and you wonder why you bothered.

You clean up the cocoa with wads of napkins then kill time in the car with coloring books and sad dried-out markers. Somehow you then lose track of time and have to rush rush to playdate pickup then hurry hurry to soccer pickup where it starts to rain. As the practice goes on and on, you allow the younger two to jump in the deepening puddles. Which is endearing until they get soaked and cold and the practice goes on longer than usual and it's getting dark. It gets really dark and the little ones start whining as if you forced them to jump in the puddles when it actually took tremendous will to be the laid-back mom who let them jump in puddles in the first place.

You are inordinately relieved to get them back home (you follow up the steps with backpacks and soccer bags and the ice-skating bag and stray shoes and the three coffee cups that have been rolling around on the passenger-side floor for weeks).

But then—you somehow forgot—the house is a sty. Which is totally overwhelming.

You pretend to ignore the mess because you are starving. Dinner is soy corndogs for kids and organic chicken for adults, but even these paltry dishes require too many pans and far too much effort.

Just then . . . his key in the lock.

You have been looking forward to seeing him all day. Because he is an adult and might listen to you. He might help you bear the weight of these kids and the late DMV registration and the fact that you forgot to buy milk. Instead of joy, though, the scraping open of the door elicits a startling wave of resentment. The resentment is intense enough to make you wonder if you really do have some kind of serious neurochemical imbalance. Or maybe it's hormones. Maybe you need to give up caffeine. Or eliminate dairy.

Or maybe you are simply bitter because you hurt your shoulder this afternoon while contorting to get the little one buckled in for the zillionth time and your aching shoulder makes you feel old and falling apart and now *he*—from the look of his sweaty gym clothes—just got in a satisfying, muscle-building, endorphin-producing workout.

You turn, pointedly, back to the sink. You are not happy about the bitterness this communicates because bitter is not how anyone ever wants to feel. It's only as you make the conscious effort to turn and kiss him when he comes around the island that you realize you want him to pull you close and hug you tightly. You suddenly want to cry like some little kid. You want to admit that you're tired and cranky and frustrated and hungry. You want him to understand how overwhelmed you are by the fact that the house is a goddamned pigsty.

Your husband, though, pulls back slightly. He lingers for a moment. And there it is: *the look.*

The look—the implication of *the look*—is almost worse than the cursory nature of his hug. He kisses you again. He lingers. It's all too obvious what he means with this lingering. He reaches, not to pull you close and hug you like some little kid, but to grab a pair of wineglasses from the high shelf. You take a deep breath. You exhale. You consider the proposition implicit in his lingering.

Only because you are years away from the dark and desperate new-baby era can you even begin to weigh his offer.

A couple of years ago, the weighing of his any move would have resulted in a heaped-up scale clanging down as you piled his fancy business lunches, on his paychecks, on his guys' weekends in Las Vegas, on his failure to be splattered with kid puke at midnight, on his inability to lactate. A couple of years ago he would have given you *the look* and you would have had nothing—not a single frivolous or indulgent or relaxing item—to balance your side of the good-for-me scale. Even in those dark baby years, though—because you were feeling put upon or self-pitying or desperate or martyred—you might have ended up having sex. You also might have felt hassled and rushed and bitter and you very well may have shut him down.

But sometimes you'd give in and you'd start fucking (in the closet or behind a locked bathroom door) and it would be all right. It would be good, in fact.

Sex in the dark baby era, though, would have had disastrous results. Like that crazy yearlong phase when any nighttime orgasm meant debilitating emotion-addling insomnia. Sex meant the kitchen would remain the crushing mess that would entirely dispirit you the next morning. Sex amounted to one kid hauling off and biting another hard enough to break the skin while you—terrible slutty mom— were off fucking somewhere. You'd then have to heap negligence onto a different scale (the failing-guilty-parent scale) next time you weighed any proposition whatsoever.

But on this dark, rainy, shoulder-aching evening you are a couple of years beyond hardcore baby bitterness. You have reached a point where you balance *the look* against little more than packing lunches. Because all three kids were in school between nine and twelve this morning and you did some good work and you've finally gotten back to the point where a cup of coffee alone in a café is something you almost take for granted. You actually had a good night's sleep last night. You can reasonably assume you'll have another tonight. You feel less pressure and malice and resentment against your husband simply because less negative baby-oriented shit has accumulated between you.

Peering through the lens of fatigue and hunger, you consider *the look*. You think: Do I feed the dog or make out? Should I unload the dishwasher or have an orgasm?

Still, you can't help but register minor incredulity when your husband pulls the cork from a bottle of red wine (the three kids happily engaged, none of them needing a thing from either of you). He turns back with yet another iteration of *the look*. The guy might as well be winking lewdly— and yet you understand that leaving the kitchen is what will pull you from your poison mood. Your husband might as well be murmuring hubba-hubba—but you don't hold it against him when he says, "Should we . . . head out into the other room?"

PART TWO

Sticky Business

CHAPTER 5

These Are Our Bodies?!
These Are Ourselves?!

Not long ago my college friend Leslie sat across her Santa Monica breakfast table from her husband, Emilio (who is Spanish and has this very attractive accent). Around them ensued the normal Sunday morning breakfast chaos, their two boys—Marco and Sebastian, six and eight—fighting over who *deserved* more syrup on his waffles, who had the better hook-shot, and who got to decide which cartoons they'd watch after breakfast.

Now it's no accident that Leslie chose this moment, with its normal squabbling, to deflect attention from the news she needed to deliver to her husband.

"Um," she began, but Emilio failed to look up from the *Times*.

"Hey," she tried again, going for flippant.

He finished the sentence he was reading, reached for his coffee, and looked up at his wife.

"I'm pretty sure," she said, "that I have warts."

The paper wilted. The coffee cup was set on the table.

Emilio stared. "You don't," he managed, "mean *wart* warts?"

But oh yes, she did. The possibility had been an utter and complete mystery, and the obsessive focus of Leslie's previous forty-eight hours.

It started with what she assumed was a simple yeast infection. The itching that you treat with a little Monistat even though some friend's doctor once said that self-medicating what might seem like a minor yeast infection— but could really be something entirely else masquerading as a yeast infection—can create resistance to important antimicrobial medications. Leslie, though, was really pretty uncomfortable. She had carpools and basketball practices and a Valentine's Day classroom party to organize. Seriously, Leslie rationalized, what mom can be bothered to get to the OB for minor itching? One night of goopy Monistat therapy, then another. When little improved, Leslie decided to take a bold step.

And Leslie is nothing if not bold. During the safe and civilized semester I had spent on a study abroad program in Spain where I wrote weekly letters home to my American boyfriend, Leslie had trekked alone through China, once hiding under the hay mounded in a wagon to cross the closed border into Nepal. While she was familiarizing herself with international boyfriends and politics and any number of Asian substances, I was familiarizing myself with lists of irregular Spanish verbs (which is what Leslie should have been doing given her subsequent betrothal). It was Leslie who chewed tobacco all through school and who had rightfully thought it would be hilarious during a postcollege ski-weekend reunion to open the door for guests while dressed in nothing but her shiny orange ski boots.

The rash step Leslie was forced to take? She locked the bathroom door and extracted a hand mirror from the cabinet. She sat down on the bath mat, spread her legs, and took a look.

I have done the same—viewed my genitalia—a sum total of once. There I was in stirrups at good old Dr. Baldwin's office. Patty, my beloved nurse practitioner, glanced up from my crotch during the second trimester of my third pregnancy and told me matter-of-factly that what I was sure was a malignant and fast-growing tumor was just a pea-size (though unappealing and unimagined) labial varicosity. Now I take great pride in knowing my body well—in loading up on cranberry juice when I feel a horrific urinary tract infection coming on, or breast-feeding at a particular angle to stave off mastitis. I was mortified, though, when Patty grabbed a hand mirror and said, "Here. Have a look."

Some years later three-year-old Xavier would take up another mirror, my sister Ellis's magnifying, light-up cosmetic mirror. He grabbed it from her bathroom counter and held it just under his package. When his little face lit up, my sister asked, "Xav. How's your penis lookin'?" to which my proud son answered, "Huuuuuge!"

Xavier would also have plenty of views of his sister's genitalia, what with young Hannah's love of nudity especially in a particular upside-down on-her-shoulders straddle position that must have felt nice and airy but was disconcerting even for a mom as committed as I am to loving our bodies.

I wrestled with the idea of repressing her spirit before suggesting that maybe such a pose would be better in the privacy of her room or with some underwear on. (Hannah's underwear having been tricky recently, though I would hazard the confusion resulted more from elaborate dress-up protocol than exhibitionism. The other morning I was helping her get dressed quickly during the frenzied dash that constitutes any school-day morning. When I grabbed a pair of underwear from the pile in her drawer she shook her head. "Those are Georgia's." Of the second pair she said, "Those are Kailey's." The third: "Those are Avery's." To the fourth and final pair Hannah said, "I don't know *whose* those are.") The point being that my daughter and her (underwearless) gang might have to wait thirty years before getting the thorough self-examination that my son, his anatomy conveniently hanging out, had so easily magnified and illuminated with my sister's mirror.

There in the stirrups, I was baffled by what Patty's mirror (fortunately nonmagnifying and nonilluminating) reflected. Folds of furrowed and dark, moist-looking skin . . . coarse black hair. I was alarmed at the idea that any part of my body was even slightly repellent. I smiled. I'm pretty sure I blushed. I nodded, though I hadn't so much as attempted to see the varicosity before I lay back down.

Far more evolved is my friend Elena. When her eleven-year-old daughter recently complained that her "bottom hurt," Elena busted into action. "I saw it as this great opportunity," smart Elena said. "I got out the mirror and had her sit down and we looked together. I was like, 'This is the labia majora.'" (isn't Elena impressive?) "'This is the labia minora.' It was great. There was nothing wrong with her bottom. We decided she just needed to take more baths."

Now my poor friend Leslie may have been told by her mother that she needed more baths back in 1980 when she was eleven, but never after having had her mother point out her labia in a bonding moment over a hand mirror. Leslie's mother, however, was the last thing on Leslie's mind as she leaned back against the bathroom wall and squinted at the reflection of her vagina. Expecting to see a little angry redness or the nasty white evidence of those vexatious yeasties, Leslie was appalled to see the surface of her labia covered in puckery red lumpy bumps.

An appointment with the doctor promptly secured for Monday morning, there remained an entire weekend for Leslie to suffer through. The cartoons the boys were squabbling over? Those specific Saturday morning cartoons had long been parentally encouraged for good (sexual) reason and Leslie had needed to get her discovery across the breakfast table to her expectant husband right away.

"Well." Emilio leaned back in his chair, his slightly hostile arms crossed over his chest. "How does one go about getting warts?"

"That's what I can't figure out!" Leslie cried.

"Uh-huh. No other news to tell me then?"

"No!"

"But they are . . . sexually transmitted?"

"I think so." Leslie then leaned forward, narrowed her eyes and said to the suave husband who worked in a prominent architectural firm with more than a few young and attractive apprentice types whom Leslie found mildly threatening. "Is there anything *you* need to tell *me*?"

"My God." Emilio's sincere disgust provided a relieved close to the conversation. "Of course not."

Marco and Sebastian were then informed that instead of

watching cartoons, the family was going to see, all together, if there was anything new and exciting out at the Pier.

Monday midday and Leslie was finally in her adored doctor's office. Dr. Stewart was young and hip, a woman Leslie waved to occasionally while walking along the concrete path that runs for miles alongside the Pacific. The minor itching had actually resolved itself (must have been a little vaginitis!), but Leslie had fixated on the bumpy skin she had seen in the mirror.

"It's so awful," said Leslie. "I'm mortified."

"You don't need to be embarrassed." Dr. Stewart set Leslie's chart on the counter and washed her hands.

"But warts! Isn't that the worst?"

"No. It's really not. The vast majority of men and women who've had more than three partners will have some strain of HPV at some point."

"Oh God. It's horrible."

"No, it's not. Go ahead and scoot down."

Leslie slid down far enough to get her feet in the stirrups but remained propped on her elbows out of some perverse need to see horror shadow her doctor's face.

Yet no more than a slight crease appeared between Dr. Stewart's eyes. She looked as though she were trying to see something better or make sense of a puzzle. "So . . ." Dr. Stewart said. "Tell me what makes you think you have warts."

"Those lumps. The red bumpiness!"

"Can you tell me where exactly?"

"Sort of . . . all over. You can't see them? God."

Respectful Dr. Stewart swiveled on her stool, grabbed a hand mirror, and turned back. "Here. Let's look together."

Leslie sat up further, knees still splayed, until she could

see her crotch in her doctor's mirror. She pointed to the wavy lumpy bumps running along the dark labial folds. "Those bumps. Right there."

"Uh-huh." Dr. Stewart allowed herself the good-natured smile she had been holding back, understanding that her patient would be relieved at what she was about to reveal. "Leslie," said Dr. Stewart. "That's what vaginas look like."

CHAPTER 6

Secrets of the Magic Wand

Just the other night Bill and I were sitting here in the living room, the kids happily engaged in a destructive and violent game of indoor soccer in the other room.

Apropos of nothing I could discern, Bill said, "You know what's key?" He was nodding, wide-eyed, as though he had just realized a foundational truth.

"What?" I sat up taller. I leaned forward. It wasn't often that Bill made statements with this kind of import. "What?" I asked again.

"The key," he said, "is the vibrator."

And the guy continued nodding, as though he was the first to articulate the truth that he and I had voiced together at least a dozen times in the six years since the original blue bomber arrived on the front porch. With more sass, more incredulity, and more irony than Bill's statement warranted, I looked long at my husband and said, "Oh really? Do you think so?"

SECRET: Vibrators are an indispensable tool that every smart woman should wear proudly in her toolbelt.

SECRET: Vibrators are really easy to purchase online. I like Good Vibrations (www.goodvibes.com). Their merchandise arrives at your home in record time with a discreet return address that reads "Open Enterprises." This means that even if your mother-in-law happens to be staying with you for the holidays and she is so kind as to bring in the mail, she won't know whether she's helping to deliver that nasty popcorn your aunt sends every year or the oh-so-festive Candy Cane Vibe.

SECRET: There is enormous variety in vibrators. This variety should be seen not as daunting, but as inspirational. Vibrators serve all sorts of different purposes. They come with all sorts of functions and intended specializations. G-spot, clitoral, anal . . . there's even one meant for the head of the penis—imagine!

SECRET: If you have a little novelty vibrator that looks like a three-inch-tall English Beefeater that your friend Ruby bought for you at Seattle's Toys in Babeland and you are named Allison, your four-year-old daughter will find the removable black fur hat at the bottom of the toy chest. Cute Claire will race to find you where you are standing in the kitchen talking with your seventy-three-year-old mother. She will shout that she has found the furry hat!—the little

furry hat for the special massager thingy that you and
Daddy like to keep in the bedside drawer!

SECRET: Vibrators are often long and dicklike and though it
doesn't feel bad to use one as the phallic object it is, and
though there's evidence that men find pleasure in watching
women do this, most women prefer external application of
a vibrator to the clitoris.

SECRET: Not one single husband I have spoken with feels resentful or obsolete or put out in any way when his wife
wields a wand. Their job is easier. Most think it's very sexy.
You can both have excellent orgasms in half the time.
Which means there's likely to be more sex. Which is good
for both of you.

SECRET: If you pack your vibrator in a carry-on bag, *no one* at
airport security will care in the least. On your maiden voyage
you will think you are going to faint from embarrassment
when the uncommonly good-looking security guard at the
end of the conveyer belt says he needs to have a look in your
bag. You will imagine that he is thinking you are horribly de-
praved. He will paw through your clothes and books and toiletries and you will blush and stammer and finally plunge
your own hand into your bag for him. You will pull out the
G-Spot Hot Handle and whisper, "Is this what you're looking
for?" He will barely look up. "Nah," he'll say while extracting
an oddly canted belt buckle that had looked on the security
screen like a miniature explosive device.

SECRET: If you are named Jane Davies and are British, you
will have been lucky enough to have shared a flat all

through university with a group of women who were open-minded and savvy and frugal enough to *share* a vibrator. A vibrator that stood conveniently on top of the television. The "tool" was to be taken down and used and carefully cleaned by anyone who so desired. Year after year the thing stood up there on top of the TV. It stayed there even when one uptight British father came to visit. Said dad acted like nothing was untoward even when he glimpsed the communal vibrator, grew red and coughed a horrible embarrassed-father cough before looking quickly away.

SECRET: If you are Ruby Livingston, you love to nap in the afternoon. You lie down in bed any afternoon the opportunity presents itself. If you drift off, fine. If not, you understand—because you are a physical therapist and your mind works this way—that in order to fall asleep you need to relax your pelvic floor. Mostly you go in for the hands-on approach, but sometimes you feel like spicing it up or you feel particularly lazy. As you pad across your room and reach into the back of the lingerie drawer, you reflect upon the intensity with which you enjoy your vibrator.

SECRET: Vibrators do not mean you are lazy. Having a vibrator does not mean you are letting your husband too easily off the hook. Having a Rabbit at the back of the shelf where you keep your winter scarves or a Laya in your husband's retired gym bag or a Cool Vibe 600 behind the books on the bedside bookcase does not mean the end of cunnilingus if you love cunnilingus. If you love when your husband sucks hard on your nipples, your vibrator will not get in the way. If you like it from behind, you just happen to be in the perfect vibrator position and you might not even realize it! You know what vibrators rival? Sliced bread.

SECRET: You may worry that you will come to depend upon your vibrator. As well you should. You might like your Wascally Wabbit or Fukuoku 9000 so much that you half-joke with your husband about putting one (along with ample spare batteries) in the enormous plastic backyard survival tub that you assembled after 9/11 then bolstered after a local earthquake and then again after Katrina (all in your ongoing efforts to convince yourself that if you pre-pare meticulously enough, nothing bad will actually happen to you). When a radio announcer encourages you to think of the things you couldn't do without during the crucial four days when you should be able to survive independently after a natural disaster, your Magic Wand will come to mind just after coffee, your bladder infection antibiotics, and the vanilla milk the kids subsist on these days.

SECRET: You might be shocked (and proud) of how quickly you burn through the batteries in your vibrator.

SECRET: You may become dependent enough on your vibra-tor that it will be sort of sucky to forget your Lucid Dream when you go away with your husband for a weekend in New York. It will then be exciting to have to remember all those old elaborate orgasm strategies. It will feel like really hard work but you'll eventually get it done the old-fashioned way. You will be pleased that you've still got it in you, but mostly you'll miss your vibrator. It may well be the first item you pack for your next weekend away.

SECRET: At a rather raucous wedding reception dinner table, a slightly shocked but mostly interested tablemate who also happens to be an ambitious businesswoman will say that she actually once did a business school case study on vibrator sales. The team cross-analyzed the number of vibrator sales with the number of people who admit to having bought vibrators. Evidence suggested that people who own a vibrator probably own not one but more like six or seven. You will smile. You will lean close and say, "There's a really good reason for that."

SECRET: Vibrators are not some kind of mechanical erosion of the intimacy between you and your spouse. Vibrators are an excellent way to add variety and ease, excitement and satisfaction to monogamy.

SECRET: Vibrator vendors caution that battery-operated vibrators are novelty items and may last "anywhere from a week to several years." It can be frustrating to have your vibrator crap out on you mid-fuck. I recommend a backup.

SECRET: You may find a sort of escalation in the vibrators you purchase. A small pocket-size one (like the bullet vibe Jane Davies's husband gave her "for her purse"!) might be fine. Such a little one will feel good. But you may correctly assume that bigger will be better. Bigger might mean a Turbo Glider Raspberry or a Gigolo, which are girthier, longer, and more penislike, all of which is good. Eventually you might graduate (try to think of it that way) to the plug-in variety.

SECRET: If you are staying at the Four Seasons in Las Vegas and you happen to leave your vibrator in the tangled bedclothes when you head out to the blackjack tables, you will return to find your bed nicely turned down. You will also find your chrome Steelworker Vibe standing brawnily on end, right between your facial cleanser and your toothbrush in the neat line of toiletries on the fancy bathroom counter.

SECRET: If you are at *home* and you happen to forget your Blue Bomber in the tangled bedclothes and it's the morning that the housekeeper comes, you will be mortified to return home to a neatly made bed. After a harried search you will find your vibrator in the bedside drawer along with coins and hair elastics and the stray Polly Pocket doll that caused all that lost-toy angst the afternoon before. You will feel seriously repressed by the terrible embarrassment you experience at the idea of a fifty-three-year-old Hispanic Catholic widow having to put away your sex toys.

SECRET: If you keep your vibrators in the back of your husband's lowest bureau drawer and your two-year-old comes rushing into the room and slams the door, she will cause the Thumper to twist into the "on" position. This will create a loud and surprisingly monsterlike rumble in the drawer that will scare the bejeezus out of the toddler who will run terrified across the bedroom to the big bed where she will be comforted by her chuckling parents.

SECRET: If you indulge in the Hitachi Magic Wand you will be mortified when you pull that sucker out of the Open Enterprises box because it's really so large. The first time you use it, however, you will have four astonishingly excellent orgasms in twelve minutes. You will then be convinced that your new accoutrement is the perfect size after all.

SECRET: The word *massager* is printed right on the handle of the Magic Wand. *Massager* legitimizes your new tool in a way that no other vibrator can be legitimized. You can store a massager right in the bedside drawer without feeling like a pervert! A massager means you will feel fine about telling your kid to grab the booklight out of the bedside drawer himself instead of worrying about what he might find therein. Having a massager situated in the bedside table as opposed to all the way across the room at the back of the sweater shelf is a beautiful thing.

SECRET: Your husband might be slightly appalled when he first sees your new Magic Wand. This will *not* be because it is big or intimidating or in any way makes him feel redundant. Your husband will look slightly flummoxed because he will be trying to get over the boyhood memory of massaging his own little shoulders with his parents' strikingly similar massager.

SECRET: If you invest in the Hitachi plug-in model (a wise move), your four-year-old will race in after you've unlocked the Private Time door (see "Talk to Me, Babies") to find it still plugged in and strewn on the bedroom floor (oops). He will cry, "Look! Hey! A microphone!" He will pick it up and sing a bar of *High School Musical* before screwing up his little face, casting down the wand, and saying, "Yuck. It smells funny."

SECRET: If you become as evangelical as some of us, you can use your vibrator(s) as an excuse to throw your own local version of a pleasure party (see "Pleasure Party"), which is a *really* good time had by all.

FINALLY: If you don't have a vibrator, buy one pronto. If it ever takes you more than three or four minutes to achieve orgasm, buy two. If you have reservations, if having a vibrator seems gauche or complicated or weird, try to reverse that thinking. Try adopting the idea that each woman owes herself one. Never fear your vibrator. Love love *love* your vibrator.

CHAPTER 7

Talk to Me, Babies

Soon after the series of erotic dance classes with Catherine Rose, Bill and I experienced failure of our stick-the-kids-in-front-of-a-video privacy strategy when five-year-old Hannah charged through a bedroom door Bill and I each thought the other had locked. Ever my hero, Bill thought fast. When Hannah cocked her fair head to one side and asked what he was doing on top of me, he tapped into their bedtime wrestling lexicon and said, "Body-slammin' Mommy."

Now. I was born in 1969 in Northern California. I grew up calling my parents' friends by their first names and had a mother who hosted naked massage groups for her women friends in lieu of bridge parties. We thought nothing—as a family—of using words like penis and vagina and I recall no

uncomfortable lecture on reproduction because such discussion was as natural as the question of who was taking
out the trash or what was for dinner. Bill, on the other
hand, is Catholic and from Massachusetts. Bill recalls no
discussion of reproduction whatsoever, remembering only
that he spent a good part of adolescence trying to refrain
from the "sin" of masturbation. Despite his Puritan upbringing, however, my husband is miraculously immodest,
entirely comfortable with nearly all bodily functions, and
not opposed to strategies that promise more sex.

Which is how, the very evening of Hannah's inquiry, we
came to establish Private Time. "During Private Time," Bill
explained at the dinner table, "Mommy and Daddy will
have time . . . to be private. We might . . . sit and talk . . .
out on the porch."

"Or," I continued, "have a glass of wine in the living
room."

In reality, of course, Private Time meant Bill and me racing to the bedroom.

So I might have anticipated the topic that arose a few
days later. There I was, secured in the driver's seat, my kids
captive in seatbelts behind me. Our most meaningful talks
often occur in the car where no eye contact muddies conversation, no games or puzzles or playdates interfere, and
only the radio distracts.

"Mommy?" Something in Hannah's searching tone
makes me turn down the music, hoping that she hasn't de-
coded Beck's "Girl" and come up with a question about off-
ing your lover.

"Yeah?" I ask.

"How *do* mommies make babies?"

Well! I am perky. Ecstatic even! I have always loved parenting moments that involve exploration of big questions like gravity, daylight savings, why it feels so sad to see a dead bird on the sidewalk. When the topic is as foundational as reproduction, the dialogue couldn't feel more rewarding. Here at last—not naked in the bathtub or beside a newborn sibling's crib—I will initiate what I imagine to be the first of many satisfying conversations on this vital topic. I will replace the single old-school "birds and bees" lecture with genuine dialogue and open inquiry. After seven years of maternity I will have the privilege of verbally underscoring the healthy reverence Bill and I harbor for the sensual wealth of the human body.

"A baby," I begin with zeal, "is formed when a microscopic egg inside the woman is fertilized by sperm from the man!" Pleased with my opening, I twist and face them, brows raised to invite response.

"Oh." Hannah gives me a vaguely satisfied smile that grows quizzical at my leering. "Can you," she asks, "turn the music back up?"

I look to seven-year-old Lucas who says, "Yeah. I like that song."

Even three-year-old Xavier appears satisfied.

"Wait a sec." I want communication. I want discourse. "Does that make sense?"

"Uh-huh," says Lucas.

"Yep," says Hannah.

My human sexuality conversations may have gotten off to a slow start, but the institution of Private Time is excellent. The kids accept our absence as an extension of date night or any other time when Mommy and Daddy are simply unavailable. Bill and I doubt they connect discussion of reproduction with Private Time, but in my mind the two

are conjoined in the freethinking approach to sex that is a
piece with the open communication and sensuality Bill and
I value. There is the uncomfortable moment when Hannah
pounds on the locked Private Time door and shouts, "Are
you guys *done* yet?" But this is well balanced by the laugh
Xavier, Bill, and I get when three-year-old Xavier knocks
and knocks on the Private Time door, finally yelling, "Let
me in! Let me in!" to which Bill answers, "Not by the hair of
my chinny-chin-chin." Just as I am congratulating myself
on such an effective privacy plan, though (heading into the
living room with a glass of wine for myself and one for Bill),
I overhear Hannah say, "Hey, Lucas. Are they having Private
Time?" to which a nonchalant Lucas replies, "Maybe. If you
want to know, go out there and see if they've got any
clothes on."

To my disappointment, months pass without any more
parental-filial dialogue on sex. We discuss the mechanics of
catastrophic Louisiana floods, the reasons Americans pay
taxes and the astounding fact that people actually survived
childhood without TiVo. Finally, one afternoon Hannah's
beseeching "Mommy?" carries distinct promise.

Turning down Nirvana's "Smells Like Teen Spirit" I say,
"Yeah?"

"So how does the sperm actually get out of the man?"

At long last! I turn with a grin to find that his sister's
query has even piqued Lucas's curiosity.

"Great question," I enthuse. "I'm glad you asked! The
sperm comes out of the man's penis." (Along with un-
abashed familial nudity, Bill and I take pride in bandying
about body-part terms like vagina and uterus, scrotum and
penis.)

"Really?" asks Lucas, his interest waxing.

"Yes!" Here it is, I think to myself . . . dialogue! discourse! "Out of the urethra!" I fairly cry as I fix my animated stare on them. "The same opening boys and men pee out of!"

"Oh," says Hannah agreeably.

"Oh," says Lucas contentedly.

I glance to the road then again stare at my kids.

Hannah looks to Lucas, who turns from me to his sister as if to say, I have no idea what she wants from us.

Xavier, in his car seat, has fallen asleep.

A few months later Bill is in the passenger's seat (I always drive, Bill tapping into an uncanny ability to nap during a ride as short as, say, seven or eight minutes).

"Mommy?"

Hannah's contemplative tone augurs a doozy. I jab at dozing Bill and whisper, "Here we go!" I turn down Wilco and say, "Yeah?"

"So when the man goes into the bathroom to pee the sperm out, do they just fly up and into the woman?"

Bill stifles a guffaw.

I flash him a winning smile, even though my enthusiastic open dialogue seems to have fostered misinformation. "This is perfect," I say to him. "This is great." I sit tall, delighted that their father has the opportunity to join in (or at least witness) this critical segment in our children's education.

To the kids I say, "You know, I'm going to tell you just how it works."

Reverting to his New England self, Bill slumps down in his seat.

"When a man and a woman are really in love, when they are ready for the enormous responsibility of having a child, they need the egg and sperm to get together. The man puts his penis into the woman's vagina!"

Squealing laughter from the backseat.

I beam, having illuminated this particular darkness. Bill sinks further from his children's sight. He looks up at me and hisses, "How could you tell them something like that?"

But this only energizes me. "Seriously!" I say to him. "Isn't this the best?"

I glance back to where Hannah's and Lucas's laughter has devolved into giggles. Young Xavier is still caught up in the hilarity. As they sigh and settle, I imagine them elucidating baffling sexual misconceptions on the playground. I see them coming to me—their confidante and ally—with questions I will be honored to answer. Surely they will become adults who love sex as much as Bill and I do.

I turn to Bill, giving his arm an excited squeeze. "Honestly," I say. "When's the last time we had so much fun?"

More important, the following weeks revealed that the kids really *had* grasped the concept of reproduction. Hannah asked me an insightful question about sperm and eggs in the instance of twins and Lucas was comforted by his knowledge of propagation when our puppy, Lucinda, had to spend a lonely night at the vet getting spayed. Not more than a week ago I overheard them sleuthing through the mysteries of mixed-bred canines during an afternoon at my parents' house.

"But so hey," Lucas said to Hannah while pointing to the crotchety male dachshund huffing in his sleep next to Flora, a young and uncommonly long-legged black Lab-boxer mix. "How would Max ever get his penis up high enough to make a new kind of mutt with Flora?"

Hannah grabbed Lucas's arm, the two of them beginning to giggle as the horse-size mastiff lurched across the lawn toward them. "Or Daisy!" Hannah cried. "How could Max ever get his penis up to Daisy?!"

A few months after we had covered this crucial lesson from the animal kingdom and instated Private Time, Lucas turned from seven to eight. Though he may not have been interested in what was going on behind closed doors, he had come to understand that among adults, the concept of Private Time could be the source of some amusement. One weekday afternoon, as Ruby was driving Lucas and her son Dylan home for a playdate, the boys agreed that it was all right that their mutual friend Nate couldn't come along after all. "It'll be sort of like the Private Time my mom and dad have . . ." Lucas grinned before adding, "Except Dylan and I won't be naked!"

Ruby—the sassy friend who had so gamely installed two stainless-steel poles in her living room the year before for the "pole work" meetings of our erotic dance series—was so entertained that she had to pull over into a fellow mom's driveway. She had a good belly laugh with the other mom about Lucas's report on our privacy plan, complete with his earnest quantification that his mom and dad do it "two to three afternoons per week."

Lucas, Dylan, and Ruby arrived home and trooped into the kitchen, the conversation logically leading Ruby's son Dylan to ask—between slurping spoonfuls of Lucky Charms—if his mom and dad ever had Private Time. Lucas thought it was "the best!" (though I'm pretty sure the nuances escaped him) when Ruby reported that yes indeed, she and Dylan's dad had Private Time too. Private Time in the Livingston household, Ruby told them, was a little different, though. Private Time at the Livingstons' occurred only in the dead of night and only behind steel-reinforced sliding doors that hermetically sealed the master bedroom just like on the *Starship Enterprise*.

That evening, having announced Private Time only half-heartedly given that a kid interrupting a glass of wine on the patio was far less complicated than a mid-fuck intrusion, I told Bill how Lucas had asked me on the ride home if anyone might possibly be lucky enough to really have a hermetically sealing bedroom.

Bill smiled, one-upping me by having learned in the car ride home from Hannah's playdate that young Brady had confessed to having a crush on our girl. "Yeah," Bill's expression held that odd admixture of pride and apprehension particular to a father considering his daughter's amorous future. "It's going to get scary."

"What do you mean?" This was interesting.

"All the boys. After Hannah."

One legendary early morning during my seventeenth year in my naked-massage-party household, our family was due to leave for a trip to Lake Tahoe. My parents leaned into my bedroom to wake me, only to find my naked boyfriend and my naked self sound asleep in the twin bed. My dad—my mom peering over his shoulder—famously uttered nothing more than "Mul-ti-ple bodies!" Clearly he was never the protective father that Bill was aspiring to become.

"It's going to get scary with Hannah and not with the boys?" I dove right in. "And what's with 'scary'? Why 'scary'?"

Bill was suddenly looking a little grim, which is always hard for me with my peacenik upbringing.

"I'm more than comfortable admitting a double standard," he said. "It might not be fair, but girls can be *crushed* by a bad reputation."

This was tricky; he was right. "I'm not saying we should promote promiscuity," I said. I may have started sleeping with my boyfriend when I was seventeen and Bill and I are very much pro-sex, but I have only had sex with two men besides my husband in my entire life. "We don't need to be super-repressive all of a sudden, though, either."

"Well, there's certainly not going to be any sex under our roof!" Bill proclaimed.

I nearly choked on my wine. He was completely serious. "Oh, all right." My voice rose as I came to the edge of my chaise. "You want them to go off and do it in cars or something?"

"They shouldn't 'go off and do it' anywhere! They should wait until they find someone they're really in love with. Like . . . when they're married."

His sudden conservative streak might have struck me as funny if the stakes hadn't felt so high. "You really want your sons to be virgins when they're married?"

"No. Well, maybe. No. But Hannah should be!"

Just the week before we had packed up most of six-year-old Hannah's baby dolls (they have since reemerged—never was I happier to retrieve a box from the garage). At the time I had mourned the passage and had worried that she—who wants an electric guitar for Christmas and is certainly being subjected to some of the nefarious growth hormone I try to avoid by buying only organic dairy—was growing up too quickly. I was disturbed enough by the image of her at some mall with makeup on and boyfriends when she's, say, thirteen; the idea of her having sex at some too-young age was far worse. I erased it by envisioning her first important boyfriend. He would be sensitive and smart. They would have dated for months and months—a year even!—before finally having excellent and intimate and caring sex (with a condom!)—just after both turned eighteen. "The important thing," I say in an effort to reinforce my shaky ground, "is that sex be a positive experience."

For Bill, apparently, this evoked disastrous images of me having sex at seventeen with someone-not-him. "I disagree," he fairly spat.

"I'm not saying we should be as permissive as my parents. I like that you have protective feelings about our daughter. The double standard is real and there's very little we can do about that."

The approach Bill and I had taken thus far—open dialogue, Private Time—felt suddenly dodgy. For us, sex meant powerful intimacy that we shared with no one else. It meant security and contentment and pleasure no matter what craziness ensued around us. It did not mean envisioning our six-year-old daughter one day becoming a floozy.

Wanting to defend at least the open dialogue aspect, I donned my academic mantle. "I just read a study suggesting that families who are more open about sex have kids who wait longer to have sex." (Ellis was the one who had actually read the study, but I needed to co-opt my sister's nurse-practitioner authority.) "And what about pregnancy? Do you want Hannah to be so secretive that she can't talk to us and ends up pregnant?"

Bill reached down and threw the ball for the dog. He said nothing.

"I want to have enough communication so I'm the one to take her to the doctor when she's seventeen and needs birth control." This was how it had gone down when I was growing up. My wise mother sensed things were serious with my then-boyfriend asked me if it was, "time to see a practitioner about birth control," and accompanied me to an appointment with Dr. Baldwin, who remains my beloved OB to this day. "That was the right thing for my mom to do. And, my God! In this day and age when women's reproductive rights are being attacked?"

I was incensed. My mother, who was twenty-five when she had me in 1969, was part of the first generation to even have reliable birth control. I imagine it was momentous for her to provide such an important resource for her daughter. I can only hope, given instability in women's reproductive resources, that I might be able to do the same a dozen years from now.

Bill picked up and threw another ball though Lucinda hadn't returned with the first. Gravely, he said, "Sex needs to be special."

"Of course it does." Even if we were feeling shaky about how our actions would affect our kids' future sex choices, this was a point we both embraced. I moved to sit next to him on the settee. I tamped down the urge to shelve all this thorny stuff and just make out. "Of course it needs to be special."

Suddenly to our right came *"BbbiiiJJJJJUUUUhhhmmm!!"*

Lucas leapt out onto the patio yelling, "Hermetic! Hermetic!" Hannah sprung from behind him, Xavier following with the lightsaber that had to stand in for the phazer we didn't own.

"Spock. Spock! Come in, Spock!" Lucas called into his clutched hand. "Mission accomplished. Hermetic seal broken." The three of them glided stealthily forward. Well, maybe not Xavier who didn't, at four, appreciate stealth. Still, Xavier's delight at an all-family enactment of anything resembling *Star Wars* was just as precious as his brother's and sister's thespian intensity.

"Private Time," Lucas concluded in his Captain Kirk voice, "is officially infiltrated. Hermetic seal broken. Over and out."

Bill and I welcomed the kids onto the settee they were storming even though this technically constituted an unsanctioned breach of Private Time. The thing was, we welcomed the diversion that kids sometimes create in the throes of sticky topics. No father really wants to dwell on the idea of his six-year-old daughter having sex one day. No parent wants anything less than a caring and intimate and respectful sexual experience for their children when that day comes. Every parent must feel some anxiety, some contradiction or concern or misgivings when thinking about their children's sex lives.

With their warm bodies piled on ours, though, with Bill kissing eight-year-old Lucas on the top of his head and Hannah sandwiched between my body and Xavier's, Bill and I ceased to be—in that moment—particularly worried.

CHAPTER 8

Arguments Against

We really must talk a lot about this for two reasons. First, you will not be prepared for the sheer variety of the assaults childbirth makes on your sexuality. Second, you will reach a point where you'll worry that your relations with your mate are so far gone that if he doesn't go off and have an affair soon you might just have to suggest it to him, to alleviate some of the guilt.

—Vicki Iovine
*The Girlfriends' Guide to Surviving the
First Year of Motherhood*

Sasha's mom? The one from the Ice Capades with the postpartum vah-jay-jay you could "drive a fucking Volkswagen" into? Well, she likes sex just fine. She is enjoying sex again now that her baby is one and long finished with breast-feeding and her vag has regained its prenatal dimensions.

But there are moments for Casey—as for each and every one of us—when sex doesn't sound like a good idea at all.

"God. Mostly when I wake up in the morning Sasha's in her crib in the next room and she's wide awake. She's right in the next fucking room and she's trying to talk to us—I have this maternal thing, this thing that I have but he doesn't. It kicks in and I say to him, 'Whoa. Your daughter is awake and trying to talk to us from the next room and here you are trying to plug me!' So he starts in with the funny stuff. He'll go, 'Hi, Sasha! Hi, Babe! Daddy loves ya!' Just yelling this crap from our bed, yelling this shit across the hallway and I have to practically roll him off me and say, 'Could you stop thinking with your wiener for maybe like a fraction of a fucking second?' "

CHAPTER 9

I Touch Myself

If parents are offended by her explorations, they'd better learn to relax.

—T. Berry Brazelton, M.D.
Touchpoints: The Essential Reference

E very mom I know has a good anecdote about masturbation. Her young son's masturbation, that is. Bill and
I used to chuckle watching young Lucas watch television
when his little hands wandered where they would. "Look!"
he would call to us. "My penis is tall!" My friend Allison
found it suspicious that her boys' pajamas all had the same
good-sized hole in the crotch, and my neighbor Sarah—
mother of four boys—spoke for all (evolved) moms when
she recently said, "It's fine of course. I just think it's better if
they do it in their rooms."

The anecdote that required a slightly more rarified atmosphere (a few cocktails and that trusting settled-in feeling at a neighbor's dinner table) was our close friends'
description of the following:

"Oh, well, that bathtub . . ." said Ellen enigmatically, when I voiced the injustice of having no tub in my bathroom, being forced instead to squeeze with my kids into theirs while Peter and Ellen enjoy a luxurious soaker tub.

"Oh, yeah," Peter shook his head. "That tub!"

"It's that Janie—" began Ellen.

"The girl loves the tub," finished Peter. "Ellen and I walk in the other night and she's lying spread-eagle. It's just about empty and the water's splashing right down on her cooch. We don't even have to ask. She looks up and says, '*Ooooh*. This feels *sooo goooood*.' "

Unlike Peter and Ellen, another mom-friend Tricia needs a less rarified atmosphere—only the trusted-friend part—to disclose this nugget about her daughter Anna.

"She jiggles," says Tricia as we rush toward our respective kids' classrooms for pickup one afternoon. She keeps her voice low enough that Anna, seated in her stroller, won't hear.

"She jiggles?" I ask.

"Oh man. It's crazy. Not so much now that she's out of diapers, but there was something about the diaper together with that strap thing on the stroller. She would sit there thrusting and thrusting and the whole stroller would shake. I would try to be the liberal open-minded mom, so I would turn her away from people and stuff. But then she'd start moaning. I'd have to stroll her away."

I find these girls inspirational. These are ingenious little kids with thoughtful, sensitive parents. (My friend Mary was less sensitive, maybe, but equally indulgent when she said offhandedly of her six-year-old daughter, "Oh yeah, Samantha's always got her hands in her pants. Those hands get stinky!") But the lengths to which these little girls go—

a slowly filling soaker tub in a liberal-enough household where a girl can indulge herself freely before announcing her pleasure to her parents, or a stroller-specific setup with diapers and straps—speaks to the physiological differences that make masturbation so different for males and females.

The fact is that a little boy's principal erogenous zone is far more accessible than a little girl's. A boy's penis is in his hands every time he urinates. All those sensitive nerve endings are right in his lap just waiting for a fondle while he's watching television or reading a book.

Not only does male genitalia mean easy access, but the general design is pretty impressive. There's the clever contracting-and-slackening heat-regulating scrotum with its truly remarkable sperm production. I will also concede the excellence of the penis for outstanding G-spot stimulation and for both literal and figurative pissing matches, not to mention fucking the newfound D-cups you proudly mash together like a porn star after the baby is born. A pair of brothers I know are rumored to provide unparalleled entertainment at the Thanksgiving dinner table (!) with their contortional "Dick Tricks." These genital acrobatics include "The Hamburger," "Towel Rack" (which involves a napkin), an unnamed one-man scrotum-penis trampoline act, "The Snake Charmer," and the perennial favorite: "Bowl of Fruit." There is also, of course, the usefulness of a long protruding member for reproduction. All that said, not many heterosexual people I know—male or female—would choose a *Playgirl* centerfold over a *Playboy* one.

In addition to a less pleasing aesthetic, having it all hang out may not always prove such a good design. On the soccer pitch, for example. Or in a wresting match with an unknowing younger sister who honestly feels bad for decades about that one time she kneed her brother so hard in the balls that she was sure he would make good on the threat that he was going to puke.

The design didn't prove that great for our friend Paul one recent Sunday evening either. For their young son Matthew's baptism, Paul and his wife, Katherine, had stepped up and rented a jumpy house that a trio of young men erected on their front lawn. The men had promised they would come later that afternoon to break the thing down but didn't show until nearly ten o'clock that night. Ever helpful, Paul ventured out onto the well-lit front porch in his pajamas. When he called, "Hey thanks, you guys. Can I do anything for you?" the young men looked at him then away quickly, clearly flummoxed by something. Confused, Paul stepped back into the house only to realize that his entire penis was hanging out of his pajama fly.

Females, perhaps even more ingeniously than males, have their reproductive organs tucked up inside. Although this makes masturbation trickier, I am of the opinion that ours is generally a superior design, what with its increased protection and greater aesthetic appeal (the latter is debatable . . . talk to my gay friend Tom or to Ruby for that matter . . . they both *love* the penis). I do have a problem with the urethra being so close to the vagina. Not that I can imagine peeing out of any other part of my body, but the urethra's station between vagina and clitoris means the poor forgotten orifice is subjected to all sorts of bacteria-laden prodding and licking and thrusting (if you're lucky). Anyone who's had a urinary tract infection knows how really uncomfortable that is.

As far as straight-up pleasure is concerned, I once read that the clitoris is far more sensitive than the penis, which doesn't surprise me. This concentration of nerve endings both argues for and against the idea of self-pleasure: such a treasure trove creates the image of orgasmic sensation being a mere fingertip away; yet such sensitivity also suggests that the clitoris might be easily overstimulated. As the girls above both suggest and counter, erogenous sensation can be elusive for many females precisely because the female genital anatomy (definitely see "Pleasure Party") is more difficult to navigate than the male. As super-smart Ellis once said while trying to talk me into a Good Vibrations Erogenous Zone Workshop, "After all, Kimber, who really understands the physiology of the clitoris?"

In an effort to better grasp where my community stood on masturbation (girls *v.* boys in particular) I began to initiate conversation.

"Have you ever talked to your kids about masturbation?" I asked Allison and Simone, John and Peter. "Have you ever really talked to *anyone* about masturbation?"

No one had spoken to me about masturbation when I was little (except for pervy Mrs. Carver; more on that in a moment). I still haven't spoken about it with my four-, six-, or eight-year-old. We've covered plenty of other topics, but I feel strongly about letting my children take the lead. Neither Lucas nor Hannah nor Xavier has brought up masturbation, and for whatever reason I seem to have children who are less busy exploring their anatomies than tub-loving Janie, stroller-bound Anna, or stinky-handed Samantha.

When I asked moms if they had spoken about masturbation with their children I received contemplative, searching answers that mostly amounted to no.

The dads pretty universally said, "I'm waiting for 'Heart to Heart.'"

Heart to Heart, I learned, is an admirable health education program at nearby Stanford Hospital for parents to
attend with their fifth-grade sons and daughters. Of course,
I harbor a self-righteous and totally unfounded notion that
my kids, what with my "open dialogue," won't need this
program despite how much I love the concept. I can't
anticipate how or when I might talk with them about
masturbation, but apparently Heart to Heart may offer
assistance if the topic doesn't arise organically before fifth
grade. Touted by parents as an objective yet accessible presentation, Heart to Heart is two nights' worth of separate
discussion for boys and for girls led by friendly MDs who
give the proceedings an I-can-talk-about-anything-with-
my-doctor feel. Perhaps more important, these doctors are
said to be "cool" even by some eleven-year-old boys who
have attended (wow, did most of those eleven-year-old
boys *not* love *me* cornering them at playdate pickups and
Little League games to ask about their Heart to Heart experiences).

One of the most worthy aspects of the program is that
boys go with their fathers. This means that fathers are im-
plicitly committing to honesty, disclosure, and dialogue
with their sons. Our friend George reported that when the
presiding doctor asked the dads to raise their hands and tell
the boys what an orgasm felt like, the fathers got a real kick
when one of them answered, "*Goooooooooood.*" These dads
also enjoyed, unsurprisingly, going around the circle of
thirty-odd men, each coming up with a different term for
penis without repeating each other a single time.

Anatomy, puberty, intercourse . . . even women's physiology and menstrual specificities caused little issue for most of
these men. Masturbation, though, proved more challenging.

Take, for example, the case of our close friend Jack. Jack is a good Catholic who had to walk away from our small cocktail party grouping when the mention of erotic dance classes first arose. (He has since warmed to that and more, guffawing as if in disbelief but seeming more than a tad interested when I suggested that he and his porn-inexperienced wife provide a little grist for my mill by taking the kids' portable DVD player into the bedroom to get to the bottom of exactly where they stood on couples' pornography.) Jack did the right thing when he took his eldest son, Declan, to Heart to Heart last fall. On the way home, Jack valiantly attempted to extend the conversation beyond the auditorium.

"So, Dec," Jack lowered the volume of the Pearl Jam he had selected in the hopes that he and his son might share a musical moment as well as a Sex Ed one. "Learn anything new?"

Declan, who had had a cursory but informative "talk" with his mother, Liz, back when he was nine, said, "Nope." Then, eyes conspicuously fixed on the road ahead and with slight hesitation in his voice, Declan added, "Pretty much knew it all."

"Great," said Jack. "That's great."

"Except . . ." Here Declan's glance swung desperately to his father's profile. "That stuff. What they said about . . . masturbation. They said every man does it. They said every man masturbates. Have *you* ever masturbated, Dad?"

"Well, Declan." Jack met his son's wary glance. "Yes. Yes, I have."

Which, according to Jack, put a stop to young Declan's inquiry, the silence in the car filled with much Irish blushing and then pressed discussion of the Giants' dwindling chances of winning the pennant.

But even this halting, uncomfortable exchange beats the complete lack of discussion of masturbation at the Heart to Heart lectures for girls! There is no mention of masturbation unless a parent specifically asks a question about it, running a serious risk of looking like the unsettling Mrs. Carver, who had once cornered her daughter and me when we were eleven and playing in their backyard. "Girls." She sat us down on a flimsy plastic lounge chair. I swear she had one of those extra-long cigarettes in hand. "I'm going to tell you the most important thing anyone will ever tell you: You need to learn to pleasure yourself before you can pleasure a man." Which was inappropriate for many many reasons, from the lack of context to the eerily imperative tone that led me to wonder how one goes about "pleasuring a man," to the more concrete ruminations on "pleasuring yourself," which led to a sixth-grader's images of an impossible one-girl "backrub train."

Of course, masturbation and girls can be sticky terrain. Several parents I spoke with were of the mind that the good doctors of Heart to Heart might seem like earth-mother sensualists or like smutty Mrs. Carver if they broached the topic. But why is this? The prevailing sense is that boys and men somehow need to masturbate if monogamy is to survive and our species is to reproduce. There is also the reality of wet dreams that boys need to understand. But why is it that we are only finding out now that having two to three orgasms per week contributes to a woman's ideal health? Why aren't more women aware that the muscular contractions during female orgasm can be really helpful in sucking all those little sperm up the vag and into the uterus for conception? Besides the fact that not a single adult I know would claim that sex is primarily (or even mostly) for reproduction. Even if female orgasm is not an absolute requisite for conception, it seems to me that girls should find out—at an appropriate age, in an appropriate context, and from an appropriate person—that self-pleasure is a possibility.

My friend Kate's friend Danielle, who teaches Sex Ed in schools across Southern California, is unafraid to take the topic by the proverbial horns. "I just tell the kids—*all* the kids—that girls can masturbate too. Because it feels good for them too." Which sounds about right. Despite the fact that the concept is presented in none of Danielle's official curriculum, she has included it ever since an afternoon early in her teaching career. A twelve-year-old boy (clearly heading for greatness in the sack given his sensitive concern for the fairer sex) daringly scribbled on his wrap-up-question 3 x 5 card: "Do girls masturbate too?" Danielle's sense is that girls will have more fulfilling sex lives if they understand their bodies better, part of which is an appreciation for the tremendous pleasure potential of the female body.

To wit, I have a distinct memory of sitting on a low iron fence rail on some family vacation. I was maybe ten. The memory of a huge sky above me suggests Wyoming or South Dakota. I was straddling a low metal-tube-type fence rail, my sneakered feet on the ground on either side. It was definitely summer: the long horizontal pole was warmish. What I remember, more than the lodge behind me or which siblings were nearby, was that if I leaned forward into the bulb-like fence post, I experienced a very nice sensation between my legs. The feeling went lost for years, though I have a pleasant memory of leaning into the horn of a saddle slung over a barrel at my cousins' ranch in Calistoga and I do recall a certain fondness for slightly upturned banana bike seat in middle school.

Not until I was sixteen, a typically stormy adolescent who retreated to the bathtub with a book when the world was uncomprehending, did I realize I could generate this delicious sensation myself. It was in a particularly soothing tub in Lake Tahoe during some ski week or Fourth of July vacation that I made my discovery. I was slightly appalled to understand that I had actually made good on Mrs. Carver's suggestion. Despite yucky evocations of her, though, masturbation seemed like a squarely positive discovery.

It did feel a little odd not to speak of my breakthrough to even my closest high school girlfriends or my mom (I said nothing to my wise and supportive sister, Ellis, who was at the time seven). For better or worse, masturbation did not become a regular part of my life. I remember feeling downright embarrassed if the Tahoe bathtub memory surfaced while I was seated at a friend's dinner table or in my sailoresque uniform in my all-girls' classrooms. The reality of orgasm did, however, make excellent sense on a boyfriend level what with all the dry-humping we'd been so fervent about. I suddenly understood that a valuable culmination to all that writhing existed for the female and not just the male!

In retrospect, sixteen seems like a decent time for this kind of exploration. And maybe most girls discover this kind of pleasure as I did—on their own, during adolescence. I do have some evidence, though, that this is not the case. My pro-sex friend Elena didn't masturbate until she was thirty. Elena finally masturbated only when she was five months pregnant and seeking a way to satisfy the intense excellent-pregnancy-sex urges some women experience. "I so wish I hadn't waited that long," she says. "I mean, I learned a ton about how to make myself feel good. I taught it all to Geoff. Seriously. Stuff like, 'Circles are good. Try thirty seconds of circles.' I think that could help a lot of men. To show them what to do. I mean, my God, what was I waiting for?"

Elena poses a decent question. Though my discovery came earlier than hers, I spent a good four or five years after that seminal bathtub moment feeling pretty ambivalent about my breakthrough. I hadn't known Bill when I first masturbated and we had been dating for a couple of years before I felt brazen enough to mention my first experience mock offhandedly as we walked down the hallway of my parents' Tahoe house. "First time I ever masturbated was in that tub," I lobbed back to where he followed me with half the duffels. What felt like a risky confession, though, was rewarded as soon as we made the guestroom and Bill cast down the bags. Happily, my personal masturbation-embarrassment paradigm was forever altered.

Bill's reaction may well have come from the fact that he hadn't been encouraged to "pleasure himself" by a sixth-grade friend's mom, or anyone else for that matter. He admitted not that long ago that when he was a teenager, he was sure masturbation was a sin and that he had tried to abstain for weeks at a time. (Elena's husband Geoff is also Catholic and may be the only man on the planet who claims—still, to this day—that he has never jacked off.)

Bill's tendency toward abstinence, coupled with sharing a single room in college with two other young men, resulted in one of the most colorful feathers in my husband's metaphorical cap. Picture a cozy fire-warmed Sanborn Library, the romantic and hip English majors' hangout. Picture mid-February, New Hampshire, 1989. My Bill (not yet mine) has just spent hours on a frigid soccer field, has taken a long hot shower (when he might have taken care of some business were he not showering with six other naked soccer players), has eaten an unthinkably large amount of food in the cafeteria before settling in on a prime couch right in front of one of the library's blazing hearths. Right across from the large-breasted and blond Ingrid "The Rack" Sorenson. What seems moments later, Bill (having fallen asleep on his back) wakes up on his stomach with a big patch of splooge on the front of his khakis.

This ill-timed nocturnal emission earned Bill quite the reputation. The very next morning a pair of pretty girls smilingly mentioned his "night in Sanborn" when he innocently crossed paths with them on the college green. I didn't meet Bill until the last week of school, but I had certainly heard of the virile guy who had had a wet dream in Sanborn. Four years later, while earning his MBA, Bill heard a suspiciously familiar tale from a business school friend who had heard about some Dartmouth kid who had juiced it up on a couch in a packed library. Bill himself has been known to say with self-mockery, when I insist on telling this story to people we are just getting to know, "Yeah, well it got me the chicks."

The point being that male masturbation holds a certain cultural cachet. It's the stuff of macho virility. Talk of cold showers, of "whacking off," "beating off," "jerking off," of "spanking," or "spanking the monkey," of "choking the chicken," "rubbing one out," "snapping one out," "turning Japanese," "bopping the bishop," "basting the meat rack," "getting the yogurt off the brain" . . . all such terms (I imagine the Heart to Heart dads could circle the room twice with these euphemisms) apply specifically to men. There's even that loose-fisted hand motion to either accompany these expressions or replace them when silence is called for.

As with the paucity of inoffensive terms for vagina (we use "vagina," though friends' terms I like are "cooch," "choach" and "vah-jay-jay." Not to mention the cute Filipino suffix *lina* added to one's name, as in "Lizilina" or "Rubylina," implying that your vag is a smaller, fonder synecdochic stand-in for yourself), there's a real dearth of expressions for female masturbation. Sex Ed Danielle employs "twiddling," which is fine but sounds a little light and somehow too Alice in Wonderland for me. Bill has occasionally referred to "tossing the one-handed salad" and has tried the absurdly male-centric "stirring paint," which—in its implication of no clitoral stimulation— seems like so much male fantasy. Not one of these terms trips off so many tongues as the ubiquitous and penis-specific "jack off."

Maybe this inability to speak of women's masturbation is an indication that our patriarchal society is threatened by the idea of women satisfying themselves! Clearly there is biological imperative in the predominance of intercourse over masturbation. We are a sex-driven species, many of whose interactions come from biological urges. Ever since I got pregnant after the single time Bill and I had intercourse during the (ridiculously artificial) sex-free month we decided to impose before our wedding, I have been a big believer in the theory that women are more eager for sex when ovulating. Our friend John, in support of this idea, finds his wife particularly alluring when she is ovulating. The uncanny thing is that John has some kind of atavistic ability to sense when Allison (or indeed, any woman!) is ovulating. On the soccer sidelines I recently asked John what this could possibly feel like. Was it a smell, a tingling, a magnetic draw toward the specific ovary of the exact woman in question? John explained that it was more of a sudden sense—this had occurred recently in a board meeting, he told me—that he's supposed to have sex with someone in the room, and . . . (here John pretended to scan an imaginary conference table) . . . he's supposed to have sex . . . with . . . (John pointed emphatically) . . . you! Luckily for his co-workers and for Allison, John is also an upstanding and smart and caring guy with more than ample self-control. We women are collectively fascinated by our friend's ability, though. Sometimes we watch him closely to see if any careful scanning and then bug-eyed responses to one of us reveals a bodily phenomenon not even we ourselves can detect (this never happens). More interesting, perhaps, are conversations as to whether John is more evolved than his peers or if his "gift" makes him some kind of sex-triggered troglodyte.

Though it's just sort of fun to consider the subversion inherent in women not needing men sexually, I have gathered ample data to support the sexual cliché that the patriarchy (despite having no language for it and supporting no education of it) likes to *watch* women masturbate. Next time you are at a slow-paced movie (say, just maybe, *Goodnight and Good Luck*, which I found oddly alluring with all that swirling cigarette smoke) with your partner in a large old-fashioned cinema on a Tuesday when the theater's virtually empty, go ahead and unbutton those jeans a little and sit back and do your thing. I'll bet a tidy sum your husband will not be ranting about female subversion of the patriarchy.

What's even *more* interesting is how infrequently women

I know, even among ourselves, speak of masturbation despite the ease with which we discourse on other sexual topics. The one and only detailed conversation I have had with women about masturbation was in college, lounging around with several hungover girlfriends, having just woken up late on a Sunday morning. All of us found odd comfort in the fact that this was the first time any of us (except my gorgeous and sensual friend Alice) had spoken about masturbation. The conversation had begun with hot men, wended to hot women, then moved on to the question of who was touching herself with any kind of regularity. Not one of the five of us (again, except Alice) could begin to rival any of our male peers' masturbation schedules. I myself was able to count on one hand the times that I had pleasured myself. One of us—at twenty-one—had never thought to. There was talk of how to do it and I remember feeling like it was important (in that know-it-all collegiate way) to share that I had had most success with my fingertips *outside* of my underwear so as to avoid overstimulation.

The summer after college I let some of this daring promasturbation energy spill over into the letters Bill and I were busy writing to each other, he working as an investment banker in New York, I teaching high school near San Francisco. Bill and I had met during our last four days of college. Senior Week was traditionally a sort of orgy during which oversexed and drunken college kids hooked up with anyone they had been lusting after but had never quite gotten around to pursuing. Bill and I had spent a fairly chaste four days together—since we were both of the opinion that sex was not a casual undertaking—before driving off to our separate coasts. The spillover came (this is totally mortifying) when I wrote my handsome new boyfriend a letter detailing how I would sometimes think about him and "touch myself." It's awful, terrible to even contemplate. To this day it seems like an odd thing to write in a letter (a letter, no less, destined for a twenty-two-year-old frat guy–cum–investment banker who was living with three other Dartmouth grads on the Upper East Side). I have to force myself, though, to retain a shred of pride in my missive. I *would* cringe if it were put before me. But I had the confidence and conviction at twenty-one not only to write a letter about masturbating, but to actually send it. The good news is that Bill got a healthy kick out of the whole thing and I took it pretty well—was actually a little flattered, I think—when my next visit to New York meant that I was welcomed into the apartment by the boys playing the DiVinyls' "I Touch Myself" on someone's cheap tape deck.

Not since college have I had a really good conversation about masturbation. The lack of such conversation came up not long ago when Bill and I were out to dinner with our friends Kate and Andrew. Kate had just gotten back from a girls' weekend at a Mexican resort where her bold friend Danielle (So-Cal Sex Ed Danielle) had tried to get the group talking about masturbation (apparently Danielle's "open relationship" topic met equal silence). The former UCSB "gauchos" had spoken candidly about sex with husbands, about affairs they were having, about aging bodies and difficult kids, but no one would touch masturbation. Even at the end of the evening when Danielle pressed her girlfriends, no one shared. Kate and Mary and Lara did, though, start teasing Danielle while walking back through the resort. They rubbed up against lampposts and strew themselves across benches where they moaned with their hands pressed to their crotches. Finally, having gotten themselves lost in the semitropical maze of low-lit walkways, they turned around only to find a pair of security guards in a little golf cart who smiled not-*too*-creepily and informed the sexy mommas that if they were looking for Hacienda Cuatro they had made a wrong turn some half-dozen junctures before.

Simply put, we need more conversation about masturbation. That way, if there is ever (ever!) a moment in a mother's household when the babies are napping or the kids are off at school, it might occur to her to sneak alone to the bedroom for a minute or five instead of unloading the dishwasher or sorting photos or checking e-mail. We need more vibrators because the right vibrator means unparalleled satisfaction in record time without all that hand cramping (see "Secrets of the Magic Wand"). We need more moms like Ruby who are not afraid to treat themselves to a nap when needed and who—when they can't fall asleep right away—understand that they need to "relax the pelvic floor." Not only does Ruby meet her needs, but she tells trusted fellow-moms about it, demystifying and inspiring us all.

Because really, there is something sublime in being able—when faced with the total chaos of children—to recall the moment on the bathroom floor or under the covers or locked behind the home office door earlier that day. While moving through an afternoon devoted to the needs of others, you can feel good about having done a little something for yourself.

Not only that, but just wait until the evening when you're shoving a permission slip into a backpack, while tying a roller-skate lace, while helping your eldest with a math problem, all while trying to focus a modicum of attention on the husband who just walked in the door.

He'll say, "How was your day?"

You'll stand from where you were crouched. You'll slow then give him the sultry look that will make him smile. "Well," You'll say. "It was a long, long day. A really long day, in fact. But I was not afraid to take matters into my own hands."

CHAPTER 10

Laser Lover

The mons veneris . . . is further cushioned at adolescence when the carpet of pubic hair grows in. . . . The pubic hair serves other purposes as well. It traps and concentrates pelvic odors, which can be quite attractive to a mate if they are the odors of health. . . . Moreover, the pubic hair is a useful visual tool for us primates, who are, after all, a visually oriented species. The hair showcases the genital area and allows it to stand out from the less significant landscape around it.

—Natalie Angier
Woman: An Intimate Geography

Several nights after my first Brazilian bikini waxing, I stripped down as usual to join my guys in the bathtub. Naively, I assumed that no one would notice how my dark pubic hair (formerly a trimmed and tidy, but naturally proportioned thatch) had shrunk to the dimensions of a Band-Aid. I stepped into the hot water to find six-year-old Hannah gaping up at me.

"What happened to your bummy?!" she cried, a finger pointed at my landing strip.

"Oh! Well. It's just like . . . a haircut," I said. Then for no good reason I added the cheery and nonsensical expression that a friend had recently used to describe Bill's short coiff. "High and tight!"

Reassured, Hannah took up her squirty fish and led her brothers in a game of trying to nail me in the crotch.

Her question, however, gave me pause. What would I say when my daughter's own pubic hair made its unruly appearance? I flatly refuse to tell any young woman that depilation is necessary to please men, that Brazilian waxings are needed to avoid unsightly hair hanging out of the skimpy thongs that have become de rigueur even for mothers these days. I squirted back at my daughter with an orange octopus, wondering at what point I would confide the reason I had gone in for extreme hair removal: Sex feels significantly better without all those pubes.

I pretty much never shave my legs. Or my armpits for that matter. I find something deeply appealing in the idea of letting my body be and I like to think my kids appreciate that message. Now part of the reason I'm no devotee of the razor—maybe a large part—is that I'm not a very hairy person. The hair on my legs is fine and blond and can only be seen (I like to think) in just the right light. The ol' pits, well, that hair's not blond or fine, but only when Bill and I have to attend a wedding or a cocktail party do I borrow his Turbo Mach 3 and take a few swipes.

Eschewing the razor may have political overtones, but I'm pretty sure that my preference is rooted less in any statement of feminist equality than in a late August afternoon the summer I turned eighteen. My then-boyfriend and I pushed through a poolside gate in Marin to find his good friend Georgie lying out in the sun. Georgie had enormous eyes and this way of slowly turning her head to take you in. She lay with unapologetic arms lazily overhead, downy pits and all. One bent knee had fallen to the side to reveal that—even in the sleek late eighties, even in high school when peer pressure reached its zenith and shaving was novel for us adolescents—gorgeous Georgie was more than comfortable with body hair.

Sensuality was thus defined for me by a certain turning of the head and this young woman's dark pubic hair peeking out of her bikini. I gave up Nair. I enjoyed telling friends (who wouldn't have otherwise noticed) that I couldn't be bothered with razors. When the aforementioned boyfriend asked me to "shave my bush" (apparently not as impressed as I by Georgie's unfussy confidence), I took offense and categorically refused to denude myself for his visual pleasure.

All of which made the shift I experienced fifteen years later so surprising. Indulging in an afternoon with my pro-sex sister at a local spa, I headed toward the steam room where Ellis warned me that she had just treated herself to her first "Brazilian" and that I was not to be shocked.

"I asked the woman to leave a little," she said as she doffed her robe. "It's kinda cute. See?"

An imaginative esthetician had left my sister's dark pubic hair in the shape of a small heart.

"Kimber," she said. "You have to try it. Seriously."

My poolside days had devolved into tossing dive toys and being forced to play Marco Polo while ensuring that no kid bonked his or her head on the diving board. My sister's proposal made me laugh. I told her it would be a waste of money. "Shit," I added, "it's not like I'm trying to impress anyone. Besides, no hair really hangs out of my bikini."

"It's not about the bikini." Ellis smiled knowingly. "It's about sensation."

Well. I love sensation. I love massages and soaks in the bathtub. I love sex. Ellis was suggesting that Brazilian waxing wasn't for my husband or poolside spectators, but for me. I considered the fact that our friend Peter, the one who dislikes lingerie almost as much as his daughter Janie likes their soaker tub, prefers a nice big bush on his wife Ellen. This was balanced, though, by our friends Allison and John who admitted recently that he likes to shave her (over a towel that they spread on the bed) as an occasional "fun" part of foreplay.

Never one to doubt my sister's wisdom, I found myself at LaBelle Day Spa the following Thursday with a white-robed professional named Svetlana.

Arms crossed as she watched me step out of my jeans, Svetlana barked, "You have done this before?"

"Nope."

"Ah-ha!" was the ominous response.

But once I was on the sheet-draped clinician's table, Svetlana warmed. Stirring hot honey-colored wax, she chatted about having finally raised enough money to bring her son and daughter from Russia to the States. As she used a tongue depressor to spread the warm ooze on my crotch, then pressed a cotton strip to the area, she complimented the subtlety of my C-section scar. Yank! went the strip, Svetlana giving little finishing pats with her cool powdered hand. Even when she interrupted a story about enameled miniatures and Czars to call out, "Behind!" meaning that I should roll over for her to access my nether regions, I felt a fondness for this crimson-haired woman and found the whole waxing process surprisingly intimate.

More important, my smart sister was absolutely right.

The extended Private Time during that evening's *Dragon Tales* (thank God for PBS) was revolutionary. Sex was . . . different. Smoother and interestingly altered, with significantly heightened feeling and exciting new visuals. As for Bill? Suffice to say he was pleased. Afterward, still reveling in the discovery, I made a quick call. "Ellis," I said. "I am forever, I mean for*ever*, in your debt."

Although I remained lax in matters of other hair removal, Brazilian waxing was like some kind of new religion. I was epiphanic and evangelistic, talking everyone I could into trying it. Sometimes Svetlana left me with a triangle, once with an Ellis-inspired heart. I've recently heard that bleaching what's left of your pubes then coloring—bright hues like hot pink or orange—is the latest trend. Given the zero chance that color will affect sensation, though, I'm pretty sure I can't be bothered.

And though I was pleased with the results of waxing, my bimonthly visits to the spa were pricey, inconvenient, and occasionally fraught. Given my negligent maintenance, Svetlana would sometimes peer down at my groin and shake her head as she took out a little comb.

"Too long, too long," she would cluck, her frown giving me to understand that this would be more painful than usual. "Next time, you trim better!"

As soon as the Easy-Laser 1600 got mainstream enough for LaBelle, I made the logical, if irreversible, decision to eradicate the majority of my pubic hair. Laser hair removal was a dream—far less painful than hot wax and although it seemed expensive, it was ultimately more economical given the prospect of a lifetime of ninety-dollar waxings every couple of months versus four laser sessions at two hundred fifty bucks a pop. The most exciting thing, though, was that the laser made for unprecedented smoothness, which meant even better sensation.

But before anyone goes rushing to her nearest salon,

caveat emptor. One evening out for dinner with our friends Trey and Simone, I was both pleased and vaguely dismayed when Trey found out about my lasering and said, "Now that's a devoted woman." Of course it was an objectifying comment and was sort of silly; and Trey was mistaken in thinking my hair removal was a housewife's gift to her husband. In addition, the comment made me a little worried about his wife, my longtime friend Simone.

Simone is legendary in our little town for having weathered complex infertility issues before giving birth to and raising three perfect boys (as well as having a knockout figure: really tall with long legs and great boobs). Her son Thomas had recently been piling out of Ruby's car when there occurred some boyish one-upmanship. Apropos of nothing, Ruby's son Dylan claimed, "My daddy has the fattest wiener!" The second friend countered, "Well, my daddy has the longest wiener!" To which young Thomas cried, "Yeah? My mom's got the hairiest vagina!" Now Simone would want you to know that this was no more than evidence of her son's competitive nature. I can verify from a weekend at Echo Lake that Simone's vagina is no hairier than anyone else's.

Turns out I didn't need to worry about Simone feeling badly about her allegedly hirsute state as compared to my newly depilated one. She set her martini down on the restaurant table. She smirked at her husband and shot back, "Well. I've heard it's not that great an idea. Down the road." She looked to me. "I've heard it doesn't always look so good. Like a tattoo on an older woman or something. You know . . ."

"What?" I asked, a little alarmed.

"I've just heard from older friends—and one who just

had a baby, come to think of it—that things start to—" Here buxom and willowy Simone laughed with a kind of glee. She made an odd downward motion with her hands. "Things just start to hang out!"

There was no going back. I simply had to believe that the laws of gravity wouldn't apply to me. If they did, I told myself, and certain unforeseen vaginal tissue "hung out," I would allow my body to age gracefully, embracing the wrinkles and sags I was determined not to doctor. Besides, at that point all was well both in the bedroom and the bikini.

The nursery, however, was a different story.

That first bath time, once Hannah was reassured that no damage had been done to my "bummy," I had counted myself lucky that Xavier and Lucas had only taken up their own squirty sea creatures and joined their sister's target practice, oblivious to my manicured crotch.

Or so I thought.

The following Friday night I was settling eight-year-old Lucas and Simone's son Thomas into their sleeping bags in the playroom. I had made them pee one last time and had watched them brush their teeth and then, assuming they were content with the falling-asleep *Ice Age* DVD they had selected, I made my way upstairs and stripped down for bed.

Where they found me some five minutes later as I stood at the sink washing my face.

"I, um. I think . . ." Thomas stammered uncharacteristically, leading me to believe he was sheepish at wanting to go home tonight after plenty of successful sleep-overs. I turned to the boys.

"It's fine!" I reassured. "You can absolutely go home if

you want to. I used to do this all the time when I was little."
Not about to venture out of the house this late at night,
though, I ushered them into the hallway. "Let's catch Daddy
quick on his way out to basketball." Not until we were
halfway down the stairs did Lucas look to me with a smile
and say, "Mommy, why are you talking to Thomas without
any clothes on?"

Of course, Thomas's mother is "hairiest-vagina" Simone.
We laughed the next morning on the phone, when Simone
quickly dispelled my theory that Thomas wouldn't have really even noticed my nudity. Thomas had already reported
the incident to both of his parents in turn. Simone and I
(thankfully) agreed that her son hadn't been scarred forever. She suggested that what was interesting about his
experience were any differences he might have detected between her familiar maternal body and mine.

"You mean how you're so tall and thin and have those
great boobs?" I asked.

"No," she came back. "I mean how you have no pubic
hair!"

A couple of weeks later I drove my brood across the Bay to
my close friend Esther's. In the locker room of their swim
club she and I wrangled our kids into bathing suits. As I knelt
to slather sunscreen all over four-year-old Xavier, he quieted.
He leaned close to my ear—thank God—pointed a chubby
finger at the crotch of an older woman changing nearby and
whispered, "Mommy. Look." I glanced surreptitiously as he
said, "Dis-gust-ing!"

My son was apparently horrified at the sight of a wider
expanse of pubic hair than he had recently become accustomed to. I lamely reassured him that "everyone's body
looks different" and hustled my guys out the door.

When I told Bill the story later that night, he laughed as I had hoped he would.

Then—still smiling—he said, "Looks like you've ruined them forever."

"Have I?" I asked Ruby the next morning at the kindergarten bike racks.

"No." Ruby, a recent convert to extensive waxing for its excellent tactile effect, paused as her argument took shape in her head. "No. Absolutely not. I see the way this thing is going. You haven't ruined anyone." She concluded semi-teasingly, "By the time Xavier's muff diving, everyone'll be Brazilian."

But hadn't I spent my adulthood subtly bucking depilatory convention? Isn't corporeal individuality exactly why I took pride at the occasional notice my unshaven pits garnered from the mani-pedi'ed moms at the park? What about the times I had espoused the wisdom and sensuality of all those lovely European women who would never dream of shaving?

I needed to talk with Bill right away. I wanted to debate Ruby's argument. I wanted to reaffirm that sensuality ought to be individual and that my hair removal choices were motivated by valid personal reasons, not societal mandate. I wanted Bill to agree that Xavier would one day love a woman for her generosity and intelligence and caring, not for the appearance of her crotch.

As I pulled my bike from the rack, though, I realized I had no phone with me. Which made me wonder if maybe Bill was working from home. I considered the possibility that he might, in fact, just be returning from a run, all sweaty and breathing hard. I imagined my husband's taut biceps as he chugged Gatorade in front of the fridge. As I imagined Bill and myself on the kitchen table, and thought of the new found smoothness and added sensation afforded by the laser, I pedaled harder. My urge to debate was being eclipsed by another brand of desire. I would think further about pubic hair some other time. I sped home, deciding that Bill and I were trying our hardest. With a little luck we would raise kids who were comfortable in their bodies and respectful of difference . . . not to mention eager to seek out the occasional midmorning romp.

CHAPTER 11

Arguments Against

On average, three years after the blessed event, women reported feeling desire about once a week, while men said they felt desire about once a day. Women wanted to be touched sexually, on average, once every two weeks, while men hungered for it two to three times a week. When we asked about experiencing orgasm during sexual activity, men reported climaxing six times more often than women! Again, this is three years postbaby.

—John M. Gottman, Ph.D., and
Susan Schwartz Gottman, Ph.D.
And Baby Makes Three

My friend John? The one who can sense when women (especially his wife, Allison) are ovulating? John is sensitive in other ways too. John is the kind of guy who encourages his wife to go away for girls' weekends. He's a man who gave up a lucrative tech career to found a local nonprofit organization that supports teens, and John can chat on the phone with the best of us.

John did display some manliness, though, when he recently e-mailed me his arguments against (and for) sex in a form—two numbered lists—that struck me as notably male. Here they are:

Top Ten Reasons NOT TO Have Sex

10. "Messiness: periods, wet spots, postcoital hygiene, all the clutter I'd have to clear off my desk if we're really going to do it right here on my desk."
9. "The lock on our bedroom door doesn't work."
8. "We have no curtains on the front windows of our house (or on our bedroom windows for that matter)."
7. "Everyone else at the dinner party is wondering why we're in the bathroom together."
6. "It's twelve a.m. and I need some sleep."
5. "We have to be in church in forty minutes."
4. "I just want a quickie, but what if s/he takes a lot of time?"
3. "I've got too much work to do."
2. "I'm exhausted."
1. "I've just finished playing with myself, it'll never work."

Top Ten Reasons TO Have Sex

10. "All the clutter gets swept off my desk."
9. "If we pile the laundry hampers in front of the door we can tell the kids we were building a fort."
8. "Our neighbors lead very boring lives and could use the excitement."
7. "No one else at the dinner party noticed me sneak into the bathroom with you."
6. "It's two a.m. and I can't get back to sleep."
5. "We don't have to be at church for another forty minutes."
4. "It's okay to ask for a quickie."
3. "Awww, c'mon. It's been a month."
2. "Allison's ovulating."
1. "Once Mr. Happy comes to attention, who needs to think of a reason?"

PART THREE

Up and Over

CHAPTER 12

Porn Wars

And the truth is that in-your-face vileness is part of the schizoid direction porn's been moving in all decade. For just as adult entertainment has become more "mainstream"—meaning more widely available, more acceptable, more lucrative, more chic: Boogie Nights—it has become more "extreme". . . . The thing to recognize is that the adult industry's new respectability creates a paradox. The more acceptable in modern culture it becomes, the farther porn will have to go in order to preserve its sense of unacceptability that's so essential to its appeal. As should be evident, the industry's already gone pretty far.

—David Foster Wallace
Consider the Lobster

Together, they head over the hill. The wide highway that cuts through tall grasses gives way to the steep and tortuous redwood road that then descends toward cliffs and the Pacific.

She's nine months pregnant. In her desperation they have dropped their two-year-old daughter and four-year-old son at her parents. They are getting away for one last night. An indulgent stay at a hotel on the coast. It's less than half an hour's drive but already, here in the car, she feels phenomenally distant from her children's clinging and whining and needing. It is precisely this overnight that has gotten her through the last few weeks. This is a badly needed last hurrah, a final twenty hours of relaxation and self-indulgence and intimacy before she is subsumed again by the dark, dark days of mothering an infant.

And this infant, she understands, will be complicated by the exhausting, overwhelming reality of its siblings. She, really hugely pregnant at this point, has not slept through a night in four years. It's with a near posttraumatic stress type of dread that she imagines Dr. Powar slicing into her body to extract the infant that she will then—*right* then—have to feed from her own damaged body and comfort largely by herself (a babysitter comes for twelve hours each week and her husband is taking ten days off work—but who is she kidding? She's been through this twice before. She is the only one who will have that baby-soothing mother's smell. Only she can provide the crucial one-on-one mother time that will see the older two through this difficult transition. She will be the only one lactating).

The infant inside of her, though, and his/her siblings . . . all children have been forgotten by the time the car pulls off scenic Highway One and onto Miramontes Point Road (the infant as forgotten as a creature pushing and stretching—feeling too big inside of her—could ever be). Her belly is truly enormous. This belly no longer elicits strangers' fond smiles. As she heaves herself up and out of the car she receives glances that say: No woman as hugely pregnant as you are should be checking into any institution that's not a hospital. Still, children evaporate in the familiar woodsmoke of the tasteful portico, in a sterling bowl of perfect green apples at reception.

They both love this hotel. She feels content here, peaceful and optimistic and amorous. They love this hotel even as others criticize Half Moon Bay for its wind and fog.

There's no pool to speak of, no easily accessible beach along these sheer cliffs. She's glad there's no scuba diving or sailing or whale-watching tours (each of which would require putting her book aside). There is, instead, a wood-paneled and gas-lit library where she will sit reading with her husband, usually the two of them alone, interrupted only by the man in livery from another era who occasionally steps in to ask if they'd like tea or something to eat.

And while her bathroom at home teems with newborn diapers (that the 9 lb. 6 oz. baby she is carrying will never fit into) and pink toddler diapers and big-boy nighttime pull-ups, and while the shelves are stocked with Extra Strength Tylenol and maxi-pads and lanolin for cracked and bleeding nipples, their bathroom at the hotel is elegantly spare. She moves slowly through the ample space. She takes up and smells the packet of bath salts. She savors the cool sandstone underfoot and fingers the pair of lavish white robes hanging on the back of the heavy cream-colored door.

She'll never bother, she knows, with a robe. She's already undressing, her ugly maternity clothes left in a black heap on the pretty floor. Not more than fifteen minutes since check-in and she's walking naked to where her husband lies on four-hundred-thread-count linens, three large down pillows squashed behind his head.

"Is this unbelievable?" she asks as she crawls toward him.

The hand holding the remote falls and he smiles at her. He nods, thinking that it's cute to see her so impressed by what had ceased—after the hundredth fancy business hotel—to genuinely impress him.

"It is nice," he says, pulling her very pregnant body close.

And because she knows that he is not wowed by the ample provisions in the mini-bar or the dozens of feature films they can order up, she looks to the TV screen and teases. "Catch up on *SportsCenter*?"

"Sure." He smiles then raises the remote. "But maybe we ought to catch up on some porn."

A decade before, this statement would have been impossible. At twenty-one she had been outspoken in her hatred of pornography. To this very pregnant day a decade later, she has never deigned to see any.

Her husband seems to have forgotten this. He seems to have forgotten that she finds pornography degrading and objectifying. Has he forgotten her rants about how the astoundingly profitable pornography industry evinces a vile American obsession with images of artificial beauty and violence against women? He seems not to recall that his wife finds the notion of pornographic film disturbing and upsetting in the extreme.

But there on crisp linens he's idly stroking her shoulder with his fingertips. He suggests porn and she says, "Okay!"

The reason being? She simply cannot get enough. Pregnancy sex has been unlike any sex before it. Something to do with more blood in the pelvic region. Related, maybe, to a marked and fabulous increase of sensitivity in breasts that have swollen from sub-A to C-cup. All three pregnancies have been like this: anything to do with sex she wants. It's gotten so that she's awakened every few weeks by resounding orgasms that leave her sweaty and breathing hard and clambering over sleeping toddlers to get on top of her husband so they can go it again. It got—at one recent point—so that he had to admit one evening when she was verging on pushy that very-late-pregnancy sex had become ". . . cumbersome."

Just watching him order up the adult feature is enough to make her hot. She won't remember the name of the film.

She won't notice her feminism expanding, in that moment, to encompass the choosing of new avenues of sexual stimulation. She neither remembers the title nor considers her shifty feminism because her mind has been hijacked.

The screen fills with a large-breasted blond woman, her fine features pretty enough. The camera captures her straight on, long tan legs spread as she fucks a muscular man lying on the wooden lounge chair she's straddling. Her breasts are large but soft looking. They're round and bouncing slightly as she raises and lowers herself, moaning all the while, slowly, up and down on the guy's cock.

There on the bed, nine months pregnant and being fucked from behind—pretty much the only position left to them—her husband seems sort of incidental. Never has her brain registered anything like this. Never in her entire life has she laid eyes on such full, round naked breasts. There are other shots, a shift to the woman's nicely rounded ass, a close-up of a penis thrusting, both of which are fine, turn-ons actually. But it's the camera's return to its original perspective, it's the round breasts, it's the way the pretty-enough woman raises her hands and presses her breasts together, it's the softness and the amplification of their size with the pressing (as well as real fingertips at our pregnant viewer's crotch) that make her come.

All of which is excellent! Just as she's about to hurtle deeper into the dark, dark tunnel of parenting very young children, porn offers her a glimmer. If visual stimulation can make her body feel that good, that immediately aroused and easily orgasmic, she wants more. If watching porn can transport her that far away from her pregnant and overwhelmed self, she'll watch all she can get her pregnancy-swollen hands on.

Quick, before the baby comes, she takes her wise sister's advice and switches from Netflix to GreenCine because—as Ellis says—"mail-order DVD services are made for porn."

Quick, while packing her hospital bag a week before the due date she realizes that the portable DVD player is useful for far more than cross-country flights.

Quick, she learns to navigate 89.com and tomsthumbs .com and wifeysworld.com. (she hates the awkward and offensive names of these sites, but she really likes the viewing). She straddles her husband in their little home office, both facing the computer screen, porn necessarily constituting an office-friendly quickie because of how fast it makes her come. In this position—not unlike that of the inaugural porn star fucking the man on the wooden lounge chair—she learns to click on the little thirty-second previews, clicking on them a few times, never actually subscribing to any of these services because of the pop-ups she's worried the kids might happen upon years later when they're old enough to stray from the educational games on pbs.org.

Less quickly, they survive the first really taxing months of infancy, which turn out to be, incidentally, not as horrifying as she thought. She is less worried about the new baby sleeping because no one else in the house is sleeping. She finds herself wanting to sit alone in her bedroom and stare at this new baby because he seems perfect and good and because he is her last (not to mention that the older two came down with a stomach virus while she was in the hospital and even she would rather hold an infant than clean up puke).

Of course there is a porn drought in these first months. That's the way it generally goes: Periods of less porn followed by periods of more. Less when the holidays roll around and there are in-laws and grandparents everywhere they turn. More when the portable DVD player happens to be set up in their bedroom for some sleepless child to watch *Jungle Book* the night before GreenCine delivers *Eyes of Desire 2*.

They watch porn together. One will say, "Hey, want to do it in the office?" which is a kind of code for porn. They each learn which visuals the other likes. They learn to add running commentaries that underscore these preferences. Once they are both satisfied, pulling jeans back on in the office or lying sprawled in a Private Time bed, they laugh together at how really silly the people seem, that pair of phony-looking strangers (so powerfully alluring a moment before) frozen there on the monitor or fucking away on the little DVD screen.

And they watch porn apart: he on trips, she during an extremely uncommon midmorning when she actually finds herself alone in the house. She will have been sitting on the couch innocently reading. She will have turned a page only to find a really well-written and seriously arousing passage. She will think to herself, "Oh, fuck. Now I have to go masturbate." She'll dial up a little porn and grab the vibrator from the way back of the office desk drawer because that's the quickest way to get back to her book.

As with vibrators, she wants to proselytize. She sits on the back patio with Ruby and Kate as kids orbit around them, one mixed-gender faction playing "Lightsaber Battle to the Fiery Death," the other, "House." She wonders aloud as she crosses her legs under her about the possibility—how convenient! how discreet!—of downloading porn onto an iPod.

"Not sure," says Ruby. "I'll have to look into that."

"Now," Kate says, setting her cup of coffee on the patio table as she ties her daughter's apron, "here's what I'm wondering."

"What?" asks Kimberly.

"What?" asks Ruby, a fellow porn fan.

"When Andrew and I were in Hawaii it was our tenth anniversary, you know? We decided it'd be fun to watch some porn. Mix it up a little."

"Yeah?" leads Ruby, whose black hair was recently dyed teal in strategic chunks.

"So we order it from the in-room entertainment thing and we're pretty excited. But then there's just all this naked flesh. All this . . . penetration."

Kate's friends stare, seeing no problems.

"We were thinking: 'Where's the pizza delivery guy? Where's the copy machine repairman? Or the French maid or the nurse or the cop?' And, shoot—'Where did all the pubes go?' "

Kimberly laughs (while privately regretting her feminist-mandated lack of experience against the wealth Kate appears to have viewed).

But generous Ruby—for whom a DVD is nothing compared to the steel poles she installed for the "pole work" segment of erotic dance—acts as though Kate were in need of life-saving medication, or vast sums of money. "I have what you need. I saw it on the Good Vibrations Web site."

Before the week is out, Ruby has delivered *Pirates* to Kate, who is unable to give any kind of report until a couple of weeks later.

"It was terrible!" Kate laughs, covering her eyes as though pirate porn were rolling on the kitchen wall across from where she sits having a Friday glass of wine with Kimberly.

"It was all this plot. All this 'Yahhr, matey!' and 'Walk the plank!' stuff. Then finally some making out. Then a bunch more lame plot. And a little more making out. Andrew was, I don't know, clipping his fingernails or something. Not that bad, but just bored with all the plot."

"Well, yeah!"

"And you know, he and I can actually bond over that kind of thing. We'll really watch what's going on with porn sometimes. Like, 'Ooooh, that cannot be comfortable,' or 'What the hell *is* that?' We really get into dissecting what's going on up there. It's like . . . porn analysis, you know?"

"Mmm," murmurs Kimberly assentingly, though she doesn't know. This is surprising, the revelation that porn apparently doesn't hijack everyone's brain. This is interesting, the idea of bonding over some kind of intellectualized porn analysis. Somehow, though, Kimberly will never be capable of engaging in this with or without her husband. Kimberly will somehow remain entirely satisfied by straight-forward penetration and artificial hairlessness and the total lack of emotion that characterizes her preferred plotless porn.

There are, though, moments. On the evenings when the glass of wine in the living room leads to some making out, or when she has been thinking about sex all day and walks by him in the hall and says, "I am so going to fuck you later." But then the kids are a total pain in her ass at bedtime and no one will keep quiet and she falls asleep in Hannah's little twin bed and doesn't stumble into her own room until after midnight.

The next morning she'll pop out of bed at her ideal four-thirty to get some sanity-saving writing in before the kids wake. But there, on their shared computer, when she

opens the drop-down menu to get to her e-mail, is 89
.com. And she feels rejected. She feels slighted and sad and
like a tease. She allows herself, just for a moment, to envision him at the computer the night before, watching
some other woman while he's getting off and it makes her
feel bad.

But she refuses to let this emotion develop. Maybe she
should be angry or sorry that he likes to watch those fake
bodies and vapid expressions, but she's well convinced
that he adores her flat-chested, postnatal self. She might
feel badly that he didn't come wake her up, but what mom
ever wants to be woken up by her husband to have sex?
She likes porn well enough herself to not even consider
laying down a mandate like two of her friends, who both
claim to have porn-free marriages. One flatly did not want
her husband ogling those artificial bodies; the other found
the whole porn industry simply too distressing in how it
has convinced all those women—daughters and girlfriends,
mothers even—that fucking a stranger on TV was their ideal
professional pursuit.

She then allows herself a different thought.

Or not so much a thought. What she allows to develop
instead of anger or sadness at his having viewed big artificial breasts and firm asses and tight abs and large biceps and
well-muscled backs . . . is a slight warming, a spreading fullness in her lower pelvic region.

It's four-thirty in the morning. Her children do their very
best sleeping in the hours just before dawn. Her husband
won't be up until six. She has steaming coffee in hand, the
silver bomber in the way back of the drawer, and 89.com
just sitting right there in front of her on the little pull-down
menu thingy.

Even while understanding that she and her husband will have to change their ways when the kids become more computer savvy (she actively hates the threat of them developing a warped sense of corporeal beauty from pornography that has never been more readily accessible), she decides to do a little viewing herself. She is empowered—her furrowed brow smoothes, she smiles a subtle smile—-as she clicks on 89.com. Three minutes and she will have erased the incipient sadness, the distress and illogical rejection that her husband's porn-foray had inspired. She will have reestablished a certain subtle parity with him. She'll feel psychologically liberated to have met her own sexual needs . . . and physically? She'll feel really pretty great.

As the site loads she fishes for the silver bomber, has a quick slug of coffee, then scrolls down to see what kinds of choices she's got.

Which is, of course, when the house erupts. With barking. The dog in the living room is barking the frenzied alarmed bark he saves only for real emergencies like solicitors edging furtively toward the front door or a particularly daring front-porch squirrel.

"Fitty!" she hisses, but there's no way this is heard over the frantic barking. She cannot yell or all three kids will wake up and they won't fall asleep again and she'll lose her writing time, which is unthinkable.

She dashes out into the living room. She threatens "Knock it off!" in a vicious whisper as she collars the dog who continues his lunatic barking.

With a hand clamped around the poor thing's muzzle, she brings her face close. Eyes locked, both are silent. This mother's body is tensed as she waits for noise from the floor above.

But there is silence. The crazy barking dog has miraculously not woken the kids. She will be able to write.

As she loosens her grip on the dog's face, however, she's semi-disappointed to realize that the porn mood is entirely lost. She will stride back into the office, maybe swearing for good measure at contrite Fitty who will follow her, and she will go straight to e-mail.

"You!" she whispers in a mock-angry voice at the pup who was only doing his job and is now busy licking his owner's flushed face. "You, you crazy dog, have no way to even begin to appreciate what you just interrupted."

CHAPTER 13

Snip!

S ay you're a man. You're in your thirties or forties. Or your fifties. You've got two kids at home. Or three or four. Or one. After several progressively more frank conversations (one particularly convincing discussion taking place in the heat of a night in a sweltering Cape Cod vacation rental when both kids are up with ear infections and your wife forgot the diaphragm but you had sex anyway and you are both petrified that you might have inadvertently created another tiny howling person), you come to agree that you really don't want more children. Your wife—you graciously concede after she enumerates several dozen torments and indignities, few of which you actively remember—has been through a lot reproduction-wise. Besides, the pill makes her moody and an IUD seems creepy. Tube tying involves major surgery and seems extreme, something no one seems to do anymore. So it's looking—the reality of it sobering, making you feel simultaneously more adult and more like a chicken-shit ten-year-old than you've ever felt in your adult life— like you're getting snipped.

Your wife might claim that you are a big baby when it comes to any physical suffering and that, like all men, you exaggerate any distress that might involve your package. But you know you are a resourceful, competent adult. You are in the habit of looking to books for information so you undertake a little research.

Here's what Amazon.com offers the day you look:

Item #1: Vasectomy Charm by Rembrandt Charms

For anywhere between $19.50 and $174.50 you could own a little gold vasectomy trinket. The first item is not the instructional volume you are seeking but an item of jewelry that you . . . wear? On your charm bracelet? Or maybe this is a present you give your wife, as if the vasectomy itself weren't gift enough?

You peer closer. The little cupid's bow is indeed up-raised. It does appear, in fact, that the cupid has shot himself, with his own tiny arrow, right through the crotch.

Item #2: *If It Works, Don't Fix It: What Every Man Should Know Before Having a Vasectomy.* (2004) by Kevin C. Hauber.

At least this is a book. You were hoping, though, for something less polemical. Something maybe by the Mayo Clinic or the good doctors at Harvard Medical School. Who is this Kevin guy? And why this chip on his shoulder? You move on.

Which is a good thing, considering the extremes with which Kevin leads off:

Will Rogers said, "There are three kinds of men: The one that (sic) learns by reading; the few who learn by observation; and the rest of them who have to pee on the electric fence for themselves." Unfortunately, when it came to vasectomy, I had to learn by the last method, which is a surprisingly accurate analogy for the sensation I experienced afterwards. Maybe, by reading this, you won't have to do the same. (2)

Item #3: *Vasectomy: Before & After.* (2002) by Dr. Lou Zaninovich.

Zaninovich—the name itself—seems suspect for no good reason. There isn't anything wrong with the name Zaninovich. It's just that you've started to sweat a little and your balls necessitate some adjustment and you feel the need to open the window because it's suddenly gotten hot in your cubicle.

Seated again, you dare to click on the Zaninovich. The screen fills with a bright blue book featuring a walnut shell into which a red pen-type tool is making a livid slice. The "nut" trope makes you wonder about this Zaninovich and maybe if he has self-published this little number, which has a cover that seems a little too cute.

Item #4: *Is Vasectomy Worth the Risk?: A Physician's Case Against Vasectomania.* (1993) by H. J. Roberts.

"Vasectomania" is just plain worrisome. Vasectomania makes you think of pyromania and kleptomania. Vasectomania suggests hysteria, like everyone is getting vasectomies despite verifiable danger. You've seen *The*

Informant and *Conspiracy Theory* and *Sicko*. You know that America's major pharmaceutical companies are built on greed and that the American medical establishment is not above suppressing all kinds of important information for the sake of profit. Damn.

(Item #20 happens to be *Is Vasectomy Safe?* also by H. J. Roberts. This item actually makes you feel somewhat better because it was published in 1978 when you were nine, so you can go ahead and discount Roberts as an ax-grinding old kook who's maybe senile and probably had a very bad experience himself. You also notice as you scroll back up that Zaninovich wrote the preface for Hauber's book—the evidence of conspiracy is mounting. Here's a scrotum-tightening snippet of Zaninovich's "Physician's Foreward (sic!)" to Hauber:

> Vasectomy is a crude surgical insult to the organs directly involved with the greatest and most profound mystery of life: The very propagation of life itself. Somewhere between forty and two hundred MILLION sperm are produced in every man EVERY SINGLE DAY. A vasectomy blocks the sperm's exit through the vas deferens. But after the surgery, the testicles just keep producing more and more sperm. PRESSURE builds up in EVERY man. Internal ruptures occur. . . . Read on: Be amazed if you will, but don't be surprised!! (iii)

Item #5: *Vasectomy: The Cruelest Cut of All.* (2006) by Brad Browns.
"[C]ruelest cut" causes such involuntary tightening of your sack that—attempting further readjustment of your package—you can only shake your head and move on.

Item #6: *London Times* Funny Medicine Cartoons: Wall clock;

Item #7: *London Times* Funny Medicine Cartoons: Coasters;

Item #10: *London Times* Funny Medicine Cartoons: Water Bottle;

Item #11: *London Times* Funny Medicine Cartoons: Tote Bag;

Item #12: *London Times* Funny Medicine Cartoons: Mouse Pad;

Item #13: *London Times* Funny Medicine Cartoons: Cap;

Item #14: *London Times* Funny Medicine Cartoons: Iron-on
Heat Transfer.

Where the cupid charm felt insulting, this array of cheap goods is demoralizing. The phrase "Funny Medicine" is just plain wrong. Bizarrely compelled, though, you click on "See larger image." The caption below the panicked blond male caricature strapped to something that looks like a large wooden cross reads "Harvis has second thoughts on his vasectomy." Although "Harvis" sounds English enough for you to feel somehow immune as an American, you look closer. On the left of the helpless patient, who has a large bull's eye on his hospital-issue pajamas, is a tall skinny doctor in sick green scrubs pulling his surgical mask to the side in a gesture that's both unsanitary and notably lascivious. With bushy black eyebrows raised, he leers, "I learned this procedure watching Ed Ames on the old *Tonight Show!*" On the doctor's left, a woman with fat red lips gives an exaggerated double thumbs-up next to a cringing male nurse and an ancient surgical attendant shouldering an enormous bedpan that makes you—there at your desk—a little weak-kneed.

You click to see the next Amazon page where you will surely find the more serious literature you need, but the second page lists six more "*London Times* Funny Medicine Cartoons" items.

Item #8: *Vasectomy: A Delicate Matter.* (VHS Tape)

The fact that there is no further description and no image of this videotape is fine, given that you don't even own a videotape player anymore. Not to mention that *A Delicate Matter* doesn't sound all that objective. The fact that this item costs $0.01 is not a selling point.

Item #9: *The Practical Encyclopedia of Sex and Health: From Aphrodisiacs and Hormones to Potency, Stress, Vasectomy, and Yeast Infection.* (1993) by Stefan Bechtel and The Editors of *Prevention Magazine.*

This item's initial promise is the cheapest of pump fakes. *Practical Encyclopedia* sounds good. *"From Aphrodisiacs . . ."* to *". . . Yeast Infection"* doesn't. Cost: $0.01.

Item #15: *21ˢᵗ Century Complete Medical Guide to Birth Control, Contraception, Condoms, Family Planning, Sterilization and Vasectomy, Reproductive Health, Prevention . . . Information for Patients and Physicians.* (CD-ROM 2004) by PM Medical Health News.

Finally! Here is the medical item you envisioned. This tome will no doubt offer a straightforward and unbiased section describing what actually happens to all the jism you won't be spouting postsurgery. No one named Kevin or Brad wrote this book; the volume was published by a reassuring consortium of doctors. Or . . . maybe not. It appears to have been written by PM Health News. You reread. The trailing off after "Prevention . . ." doesn't bode well. Then there's the use of "sterilization," which always sounds barbaric, not to mention its apposition with "vasectomy," which feels redundant. And if this book is "Information for Physicians" maybe it's not actually written by physicians. And wait, it isn't even a book at all. It says right there: CD-ROM. Fuck.

Item #16: *St. Elsewhere*.

St. Elsewhere seems like centuries ago. In part because of *Grey's Anatomy* and *Scrubs*, neither of which you actually watch. But the presence of *St. Elsewhere* in this list makes you feel like no modern information on vasectomy exists anywhere. You glance at the little image representing a "digital-download" item, and though you suspect this must be a vasectomy episode of *St. Elsewhere*, you're pretty sure no pertinent data will be found in a nighttime soap from 1982.

Shocked that you've spent this much time and are on Item #16 and have found nothing helpful, you decide to navigate to Wikipedia, where you apparently should have gone in the first place. What self-respecting man's going to read a whole book on vasectomy anyway, even if you did leave it in the can and devote only those hours to it? You sit back a little defiantly in your office chair. You type in "vasectomy," only deigning to scan for the important words that stand out conveniently in vivid blue. When the second word (after "vasa deferentia") is "castration," you mutter, "Fuck," and decide that the only information you ever needed to feel better about getting fixed is to be found at espn.com.

_____

If you are my husband, Bill, you never would have so much as glanced at any of the above despite the fact that your wife had three complicated C-sections and was told by her doctor that she should not have any more children. "Jags," as his many patients mysteriously refer to Dr. Powar, delivered this significant information—"this needs to be your last child"—while standing with one foot braced on the operating table, hands gripping the forceps. (I saw none of this from where I was strapped to the operating table. I did, however, hear the "last child" pronouncement, which sounded fine by me, followed by an ultra-loud and stran-gled, *"aaAAAArghhhh!"* When I asked Bill, "What was that?" my husband simply answered, "Jags.")

Bill is that guy who refers to vasectomy as "getting snipped" and is genuinely likable enough that friends who have recently undergone the procedure are not completely pissed off when he asks, "Man-boobs growin' in yet?" My husband is the one who, when pressed toward the opera-tion at a dinner party, will answer, "Not gonna happen." This is the guy who fainted when he once cut his finger building a ziggurat in fourth grade and has more stories than anyone should ever have about throwing up in ele-mentary school. Bill is the business traveler who has passed out cold in the aisles of airplanes (lurching toward the bath-room where he planned to puke) no less than three separate times in the fifteen years I have known him.

Now man-boobs are pretty clearly a joke. What presented more ambiguity recently was our friend Sean's comment. Last spring Bill and I left the kids with my mom and met up with college friends for an engagement party in the back room of a restaurant in the East Village. As conversations among Bill and his late-thirties comrades are wont to, the talk turned to vasectomy. Our friend Goon, who has no kids and isn't married but really likes his women, was egging things on. One father of three admitted, in the blasé tone of post-procedure men, that he had done it and it was "no big deal."

"Yeah," said our handsome friend Sean. "You're one brave fucker." Sean nodded solemnly. "No one's diverting semen out my ass."

"I heard frozen peas are important," an ex-lacrosse star interjected. "Frozen peas, a twelve-pack, and a lot of sports spectation all lined up for a long weekend."

Bill, though—whom I had just forced through comprehensive vasectomy education—was still staring at Sean. "Hold on. Sean. What did you just say?"

"They divert the semen out your ass."

This attracted the disdainful attention of the post-vasectomy friend. "No they don't."

"You mean to tell me," said Bill, who is generally at his finest with his college friends, "that after a vasectomy, you shit cum?"

Bill then promptly shared the truth—that sperm, which makes up only part of the ejaculate, is simply reabsorbed—but Sean's misunderstanding led to a thorough listing of the inevitable rumors surrounding the procedure. Bill and his friends just can't seem to get enough of the story about the infected testicles that blow up like "two fucking grape-fruits," the guy whose anesthesia "didn't take" who then experienced excruciating torment for days and days, or the guy who went back to work on Monday only to pass out in the main hallway from pain or embarrassment or whatever (only vague conjecture is offered).

Bill was downright merry when he arrived home from a

recent business dinner with a British CEO. The powerful (and clearly very evolved) Brit claimed that no one in the UK would ever admit to a vasectomy (though the UK actually has a higher rate: 18 percent of males between twenty and thirty-nine, than the U.S., which claims 12 percent). The guy went on to explain that anyone who gets "the cut" is called "a gaffer," a gaffer being a small seedless tangerine. "Get it?" asked an animated Bill as if I were a moron, "a gaffer is *seed*less?" Apparently, anyone dim enough to confide in his best friend that he had undergone vasectomy could expect to open his work locker the following morning and have dozens of "gaffers" tumble out onto him.

Perhaps surprisingly, I've never heard Bill (or any of his vasectomy-phobic friends) allege what seems logical in their weird world: that tampering with a man's genitalia might reduce libido or create an out-and-out inability to get it up. Apparently there are lines that not even good college friends cross. I keep half-wishing one of them would, but even without provocation, I've been known to shout out the fact that men who undergo vasectomies often see a marked increase in frequency of intercourse—an absolute revolutionizing of their sex lives in some cases—because neither party is concerned about inadvertent pregnancy.

The problem is that my interjections are opposed by all manner of ridiculous speculation, which is then promoted by the body of literature available to men who feel like reading up on the procedure (Bill has spent the last week shouting, *"See!"* from the bathroom where he has taken to reading the vasectomy literature I purchased. "This guy Hank right here is totally clear about this: If you get the snip, you get lung cancer.")

Indeed, publishers such as Infinity and Sunshine Sentinel

Press, Incorporated—whose self-proclaimed mission is "To Inform and To Warn"—are the proud publishers of Zaninovich and H. J. Roberts, respectively. The inflammatory "Table of Contents" in Roberts's slim volume includes such zingers as "II. Vasectogate: The Information Blackout; III. The Vasectomy Epidemic; and IV. The Vasectomy Crusade" (3). I simply couldn't get any further than the epigraphs with which Roberts opens, the final of four being this treasure: "What happens if we physicians are motivated to say something hopeful that turns out to be untrue? Will patients continue to believe us? Why should they? The answers to these questions vary with the circumstances, of course. Certainly, the stakes are high—trust and cherished social credibility". (7)

The actual procedure—undergone by fifty million men worldwide (according to vasectomy-information.com)—is so simple that it warrants no more than a short paragraph in George C. Denniston's nonpartisan *Vasectomy* (Item #24 in today's Amazon.com search).

> [The doctor] will identify the vas. When he finds it, he will gently bring it up to the surface, two full inches above the testicles, and hold it with the fingers of one hand while he injects the anesthesia under the skin with his other hand using a very small needle. When this is complete the man should feel nothing; the doctor can comfortably make a small incision, bring the vas out, cut it, burn it or tie it, cover one of its ends, and replace it. Then he must repeat this on the other side. (41)

Denniston's sane and well-balanced book does suggest the importance of careful evaluation because vasectomy "should be considered permanent" and because "[s]ome minor complications [bleeding and infection] can occur. In the hands of skilled doctors, they occur in about 3 percent of cases." Denniston's straightforward description of the procedure fortified Ellis's nurse-practitioner reaction when I expressed surprise that Bill and I would have our vasectomy consultation with an NP not an MD. "Oh God," my sister dismissed my incredulity at not meeting the urologist until moments before the surgery. "Vasectomy is one of the simplest procedures in medicine."

When prodded, the quiet majority in our circle will tell you that vasectomy—once the man makes his decision—is a nonevent. Not long ago I yelled down the hall to my talented and affable contractor, Mark. Mark has four kids, the youngest being twin boys who are eight. As he came toward our little home office I called, "Hey, Mark! Did you get a vasectomy?"

He stuck his head in the doorway.

"Yes," he nodded. "I sure did."

"Mmm-hmm," I said, waiting for further comment.

"You know, the real issue is to get your mind around the idea" (which, again, seems medically minimal compared to having your cervix dilate ten centimeters or your uterus sliced open so a person can emerge from your body). "Once you accept it, it's nuttin'." Mark paused. "No pun intended."

Nick Thompson, Jonathan Yalom, Tom Porter (who "took care of it" without even really consulting his wife Tess, who was still in the hospital having given birth to their fourth child), Blake Rush, Charlie Paver (whose only point of reference when they told him to shave his crotch was a previous shoulder surgery that had required shaving his entire torso and who claims he probably "went a little crazy" with the razor when asked to shave his "scrotal area"), George Frazier, John Lewis, Jim Reiser (whose wife Stephanie developed a convincing little mantra, "sex for one 'til you get it done"), David Young, Steve Gratz, Chris Cuthbertson, Phil Redmond . . . they're all men I know who've gotten vasectomies with no problem whatsoever.

Not that this is exhaustive evidence, and clearly it's anecdotal. But the truth (again) is that 50 million men get vasectomies every year and no more than 3 percent have even minor complications. Statistics, though, are not exactly at the heart of anyone's vasectomy decision. When Jags told us that Bill and I shouldn't have any more kids, an interesting thing happened. I felt relieved. This surprised me because I had always wanted four kids. The three I had, though, turned out to be more demanding than I had anticipated—happy and bright and fun, but exhausting. I had also failed to anticipate how much I would need intellectual stimulation and adult interaction to feel my best and to mother my children well. Four suddenly seemed like too many.

Bill's reaction was different. He was disappointed and, I think, sad. He claims to be fine with three kids and will admit that he feels "less diluted" with three instead of the four we had always planned (On the way home from the hospital with infant Hannah, the guy appalled me by saying, "Two down, two to go."). Bill is, though, the kind of playful and genuinely adoring father who should have many children. He not only coaches soccer and basketball and baseball but spends virtually all his free time on the patio playing Polly Pockets or Barbies or on the lawn playing Hide and Seek or Colors or Kick the Can (I am the mommy "who does not play" and can usually be found inside the house).

Just yesterday, to wit, Bill flew down to Disneyland with Xavier for the day. Just the two of them. The weeks leading up to the trip (the same jaunt he had made with Lucas and then with Hannah when each turned three) were filled with intricate renderings of Magic Kingdom maps, elaborate dress-up, and a multitude of fantasy scenarios in which a falsetto Bill was a far more beneficent Ariel than I ever could have been had I ever agreed to play. The thing that is incomprehensible to me is that Bill really honestly had an amazing time . . . even on the plane rides during which he and Xavier played nonstop Tic-Tac-Toe and sucked down Sprite.

Despite my husband's parental desire, I still wanted to explore vasectomy. I bolstered my case with statistics (provided not by *The Cruelest Cut of All* or dontfixit.org or the "DIY Do It Yourself Vasectomy 5 Piece Magnet Set," item #3 on a recent Amazon search, but by well-designed studies that Ellis, NP, had secured for me). My argument ran that when a well-done vasectomy is reversed within the first six years, there results a 90 percent patency rate (patency meaning sperm in the ejaculate). This means that Bill would have a solid, statistically validated chance of impregnating me if we decided in the following six years that Jags's ominous mention of "serious lifetime bladder and bowel issues" for me was worth another child. Our lives had gotten downright easy. The kids were three, five, and seven. Even Bill admitted soon after Xavier's third birthday that the trio was getting old enough to create an odd gap between them and a sibling. (I dismissed out of hand the argument that Bill might want to have another family with another woman if he and I split up or if I died. I'm too self-ish for the former and I have too much conviction about our marital stability. If I keeled over, I'm of the mind that my kids would really not need Bill to be distracted by a crop of half-siblings.)

The way I positioned it in the weeks before I actually dragged Bill to the urology appointment was that doctors were withholding an important fact: the 90 percent pa-tency rate. Again, 90 percent of men who have a vasectomy reversed within the first six years will stop (in Bill's words) "shooting blanks." What doctors prefer to give is the rate of pregnancy after reversal, which is closer to 50 percent. There are many reasons for this lower rate, principal among them the incidence of older female partners (second wives, or first wives who're exercising women's age-old preroga-tive to change their minds and try for one last baby). Viable sperm, after all, is only half (or less?) of the equation.

The other prong of my vasectomy campaign derived from the reproductive trauma I had been through. There had been four pregnancies, the first ending in the miscar-riage that was particularly brutal because we had no health insurance and I had to wait two bloody, wrenching weeks for the D&C. This harrowing pregnancy was followed by depression and desperation before three subsequent preg-nancies resulted in delivery by cesarean section. After each C-section I could take nothing stronger than Tylenol because I am fatally allergic to all narcotics, anti-inflammatory drugs, and aspirin. (When the idea of tube tying [and boob jobs] come up I still use the excuse, "I'm not a good candi-date for elective surgery.") I had spent half a dozen years on the pill followed by all the goopy trappings of di-aphragms (with which I once got pregnant). I had long been shouldering the contraceptive load. I had friends who loved their IUDs and though I thought it was Bill's turn, I had agreed to try that method. As far as Bill was concerned, the IUD was the answer. The IUD would work well for Bill.

It was after I *expelled* the second IUD that I trucked us down to the urologist. (A physician had tried to insert the first and had failed—to the tune of several hundred dollars and a discarded contraceptive device; the next OB thought she had gotten it in, but apparently hadn't because over the period of a month—my God, was *that* painful—the fucking thing worked its way back out.) It was Bill's turn. I was done.

The nurse practitioner with whom we had our pre-procedure conference, though, was of a different mind.

She dropped her chin and slumped in her swively chair. "You aren't *sure* you don't want more children?" She seemed less incredulous than disgusted, as though Bill had just admitted to tracking dog shit into her fancy office.

"My understanding," I busted in with, "is that there is a 90 percent patency rate if the vasectomy is reversed within the first six years."

She looked to me with increasing scorn. "The rate of pregnancy after reversal is *far* less than 50 percent." (Her snotty emphasis on "*far*" really undermined her argument for me. If it was so *far* below 50 percent, wouldn't she have said 45 percent or 40 percent?) Her emphasis, though, sent Bill in the other direction. He gaped at me.

"The pregnancy rate," I focused on the set of facts the NP had just sidestepped, "is different from the patency rate. The thing we should consider when thinking about this procedure is patency: the presence of sperm in the ejaculate, not pregnancy, which involves many other factors. The important thing here is that the patency rate after reversal is 90 percent within the first six years." (Bill accuses me of loving to throw "patency" into any and every vasectomy conversation to make it sound like I know what I'm talking about. In no conversation did this seem more critical than here with the professional who—it seemed— would make or break the decision.) "*Provided*," I countered with a little emphasis of my own, "that the procedure is both done and undone by a skilled physician."

Nurse Ratchet dodged again. "I'm going to go ahead and palpate the testes to see if you might be a good candidate. Just *in case* you happen to decide you want to go through with it."

My poor husband. Not only was there the surprise of having his testes fondled by this witch, but she had created the added pressure of this being a challenge, that of his being a "good candidate," which surely smacked of high-stakes business interviews for Bill.

I was frustrated enough to clam up while the nurse snapped her latex gloves and gave a stern look to Bill who asked, "Here? Now?"

She nodded.

He stood.

He dropped his khakis and right through his boxers she grabbed and noodled his balls (The fact that he was clothed somehow made the situation all the more awkward, his pants bunched around his ankles and his wrinkled shirt tail appearing vulnerable, the clothes combining with the high emotion in the room to make for a dismayingly non-clinical moment).

"You," she announced as she stripped off the gloves and flung them into the trash can she popped open with her foot, "have a very palpable vas."

Which Bill, though he ultimately declined the procedure (and no wonder), likes to announce proudly in certain circles, as if a "very palpable vas" were a goal he had spent years struggling to achieve.

But here's the thing. Only now, only when Xavier has just turned five and is kindergarten-bound am I finally coming to understand Bill's reservations. I find myself carrying Xavier more in the past few months, despite the fact that he weighs almost fifty pounds. I love the way he presses his soft cheek against mine. He smells delicious and he plays with a strand of my hair and I'm enchanted by the little rhyming strings of words he intones un-self-consciously into my ear. When I drop him off at preschool these days I find myself re-examining those cynical judgments I made about moms who weep when finally giving away the maternity clothes. As his "graduation" approaches, I find myself thinking about Bill and me sitting on the little chairs at Hannah's and Lucas's preschool "graduations." I had sat thinking snarky thoughts about all the parents with camcorders and digital cameras slung over their necks who had aawwwed away around us. I sat fantasizing about the innumerable freedoms kindergarten promised (I had gone back to venerable Dr. Baldwin after the urology disaster; he must've been eighty when he effortlessly inserted the IUD with which I am now very happy). But Bill, next to me on his little chair, had probably been wishing that we had remembered the camera or that we knew how to operate the camcorder. I'm not sure he bought into my theory that multimedia capturing of an event means you are not fully engaged in said event. Bill was undoubtedly more affected by those preschool graduations than I. He had never shared my outspoken envy when neighbors slightly our senior said they were going to dinner and a movie while we were heading into a long Saturday night of bath and bed for our urchins. Bill has been less overwhelmed and has put in fewer hours, but he is also more fun-loving and easy-going. His desire to sit alone and read silently for hours on end has a less obsessive quality than mine. My husband finally balked at the idea of vasectomy because he revels in the chaotic wrestling/mess-making/candy-scarfing/pinning-a-sibling-down-and-farting -on-her-head moments that mostly stress me out.

Now, though, our youngest child doesn't need me quite so much. Xavier claims to love Padme Amidala as much as he loves me (Bill also has a thing for Natalie Portman—must be genetic). Our youngest boy is suddenly wearing size one sneakers and those sneakers actually stink. I don't want a prolapsed bladder or nine more bruising attempts at the insertion of a pre-C-section IV, but as I kiss dark-headed Xavier good-bye and he runs off with his soccer buddies without so much as a glance back, I understand my husband not wanting to undergo a "permanent" procedure. Only now that we no longer have a baby or a toddler—not even a pudgy preschooler, really—am I beginning to admit that Bill's reluctance was entirely justified.

CHAPTER 14

Snap!

Women, like all female primates, have two basic goals: to control their reproductive lives and to have access to resources. A woman who is prevented from doing either is less free than a female chimpanzee or gorilla.

—Natalie Angier
Woman: An Intimate Geography

liza B. hadn't seen Tucker since school. He was coming down to Philadelphia for the fling they'd somehow never pulled off during Senior Week. He stayed in her snug little apartment off Rittenhouse Square for four days, during which time they had sex seven times. It was the fourth time, an inebriated and outstanding multi-orgasmic romp after a night out, when the condom snapped. Neither Tucker nor Eliza noticed until they were finished. Tucker went to peel the thing off and both were stunned to see his ruddy penis with no more than an elastic band—like the bottom of a balloon—strangling its base.

There was never any thought. Not really. Eliza had never, not once in her life, babysat. She was twenty-three and not in love with Tucker. She was in love with the liberty of her own apartment and the challenges of her paralegal job at a prominent Philadelphia law firm. Eliza wasn't sure she ever wanted to marry. "Settling down" sounded like a life sentence and the idea of an infant being completely dependent upon her was some kind of nightmare. Eliza wasn't sure she ever wanted children.

The only moment of guilt—not doubt—came as Eliza walked into Old World Coffee the morning her period was officially one week late. She was meeting the friend she would need to confide the whole mess to if there actually turned out to be a mess (here Eliza prayed to the God she didn't believe in). Eliza's friend Kimber was the only friend in town who had a real doctor. And Kimber professed to love her doctor because Dr. Gervais had seen her through a D&C after the wrenching and depression-inducing miscarriage of the baby Kimber had been so desperate to have. Eliza felt guilty because she would have to tell her sad, longing-for-a-child friend that she needed to see Dr. Gervais for an abortion.

She will never forget the book she sat reading on the edge of the bathtub while waiting for the pregnancy test to spell her fate: *I Was Amelia Earhart*. Eliza wasn't reading exactly. Her eyes roamed over the same few sentences again and again. She sat with knees pressed together, her bare feet flat on the cool tiles of her snug apartment's bathroom while she waited the interminable eight-to-ten minutes.

It will later strike her as odd that she cannot remember buying this first pregnancy test. She will remember every single pregnancy test that she buys years later when she is married and happily settled and suddenly desperate for a baby. Eliza will be unable then—during the course of those first fifteen married months—to conceive. She will never fail to think, as she buys each EPT, that it's actually brilliant how the pregnancy-test people manage to have each woman in their advertisements look as though she will be equally delighted if the test is negative or positive. Eliza understands both. The result of a pregnancy test, she marvels, is never met with indifference. She will remember the books she reads while waiting—*Ellen Foster*, *The Gardens of Kyoto*—crying this first time at being pregnant, crying later because she isn't. Married and settled at thirty-two she becomes convinced that fifteen months of negative pregnancy tests is retribution from the God she doesn't believe in for having had an abortion.

But that first time in Philadelphia she was reading *I Was Amelia Earhart* without comprehending a word. At the sight of two dark lines she sobbed. She did not call Tucker. She didn't love him and he might have been an ass. She wanted to call her best friend Theresa who had had an abortion exactly a year before, but Theresa was in the Adirondacks for the weekend and not reachable by phone. Eliza was going to be late for work at the law firm for the first time ever, which felt awful. She washed her face and gathered her things. Still crying, locking the door to the little apartment behind her, she wished she could have called her mother.

Eliza had always assumed that she would call her mom if she ever ended up needing an abortion, despite the fact that she is adopted. Eliza has no known biological relations, which came to mind when she thought about calling her mother. But the idea that she might finally become a biological part of a cosmic whole felt like little more than intellectualization because there was no way she would have this baby. She had considered only abstractly that her mother—who had tried and tried and never given birth to a baby—would be sorry that Eliza was having to go through this. Her mother was her mother, though. They were extremely close and Eliza wanted to call. But there was no way. Not because her mother would have been angry or would have tried to convince her otherwise, but because her grandfather was staying with her parents and was due to have surgery the very next day. If Eliza's mother knew what Eliza was going through, she would have absolutely gotten on the next flight to be with her daughter and how on earth would Eliza's mother have explained that to Eliza's father and grandfather?

In the leafy center of Rittenhouse Park she tells her friend Kimber.

"I need—." Eliza's downturned mouth quavers, her eyes fill, she looks away then back. "This is hard to say to you."

"What?" Kimberly masks alarm by stepping closer to her friend.

"I need to have an abortion." Eliza wipes at tears with the backs of her hands and Kimberly pulls her friend to her chest. Clutched tightly, Eliza says quickly, wanting to get it out: "Does Dr. Gervais do that? Can I go see him?"

Across the desk in Dr. Gervais's well-appointed office Eliza surprised herself with yet more tears. Not for the baby but because Eliza had sensed from the softness of his voice and the way he had placed a hand at her lower back when showing her into his office that this man was kind and generous.

"You must think," Eliza wept, "that I am a terrible person. That I'm irresponsible and immoral and a slut."

"Look." His voice was soft but resolute. As he reached

across the desk and gripped her hand, Eliza registered the childish fantasy that this man was actually her biological father.

"I don't think any of those things," he told her. "I perform a couple of these a week. I believe that if you are not ready or willing to give birth to a baby—for whatever reason—that you shouldn't have to."

And she loved him. She loved Dr. Gervais a thousand times more than she loved Tucker (who had said, when she finally called and told him that she was pregnant and about to abort the baby, "Are you sure this is what we should do?" but with hollow fear and the kind of asshole edge to his voice that made Eliza sure he had said it only because he thought he was supposed to). The fact that she would eventually deliver her two children in another city with an obstetrician who was not Dr. Gervais would be seriously disappointing. Eliza still, to this day, sends him Christmas cards.

The most salient memory of the actual procedure (aside from deep daughterly love for Dr. Gervais, whose compassion and competence grew even behind his surgical mask and his greenish cloth cap) was Eliza's lifelong and paralyzing fear of needles. The procedure itself wasn't too painful. Nothing about the recovery was too awful. She remembers thinking that the loving nurses who glanced at her chart or to her wristband must have felt sorry for her.

And she was disarmed when the male nurse who must have been seven feet tall asked if she knew her partner's blood type. Eliza couldn't have told them Tucker's birth date or his favorite color.

"I have no idea."

"All right then, hon." A different nurse, the one with the

lovely wrinkly round face, then said, "We're going to go ahead and give you an injection of RhoGAM."

At which Eliza began to cry. "I thought I was done with needles." She cried little-kid tears. "Please. Can't I be done with needles?"

"I'm sorry, sweetie." Surgical instruments clanked around her, water rushed into a sink and the order for the RhoGAM was passed from one nurse to another. The lovely wrinkly face came close to weeping Eliza, who is five-foot-two and slight, and who looked awfully small to the orderlies and the nurses moving around the hospital bed. A warm hand squeezed Eliza's arm. "Punkin. It's only this one last injection. You need this one, sweetie pie. This is the one you need so when you get pregnant for real you won't make antibodies that fight the baby."

Eliza, still weeping, nodded her head bravely. She sniffed, amazed that this nurse could be thinking such hopeful thoughts.

All she wanted afterward were McDonald's french fries. Kimberly had borrowed a car to drive her to the hospital and had been waiting and was not in the least resentful that Eliza was aborting a baby only months after she had lost one. Kimberly had sat sipping bad coffee in the hospital cafeteria, worrying for her friend but also feeling moved that she was the one Eliza had turned to. Eliza wanted fries so they drove all the way across town in the rare intimacy of friends moving through trauma together. Eliza waited in the car, unspeakably thankful when Kimberly emerged with not only Quarter Pounders and large fries for each of them, but with vanilla shakes that Eliza hadn't thought of but that tasted delicious.

A decade later it astonishes Eliza that she can't remember

the date of the abortion. For years after—four or five at least—she had made an asterisk on her calendar on that March day. Those ten years later she thinks it through and says that she made the little mark not because she felt horrible guilt or as a kind of memorial or penance but because she knew at some point the abortion would stop feeling so pivotal and she would be able to stop making the mark.

She's not even sure when that happened. Maybe when she met and married a man she loved. Yes. Then. The same point that marked the beginning of fifteen months of not conceiving. She finally gave birth to a boy and then a girl (ashamed that she cried when that second EPT was positive, not because she didn't want another baby, but because she was overwhelmed by her one-year-old and loved her job at a dynamic publishing house in New York City and didn't want this second baby so soon).

And Eliza's children look exactly like her. She pushes the stroller down Columbus Avenue and the drycleaner or the grocer pinches a fat baby cheek and tells her that her son or her daughter—both of them!—are her spitting image. She doesn't think all that pointedly about fitting into the web of biological relationships that had seemed so vital throughout her life. She doesn't, in the moments when people remark upon her kids looking exactly like her, think about the pregnancy she terminated. She talks about the abortion relatively freely and is still surprised both by how many women she knows have had one and by how an equal number seem totally shocked at the idea.

It's when her children are in the tub and their fine hair is wet and away from their faces that she recognizes her own features. She looks at them and marvels. She then sees her husband in her son's expression and this, too, seems amazing and right. But the expression she recognizes just then is one of mischief and her son is lunging there in the tub for her daughter. Her two babies—because they are one and barely two—are sitting in four inches of water, which leaves no time for reflection upon biological relations, much less the importance of a woman's choice.

Eliza scoops up the one-year-old, who shrieks at being lifted from the warm water. She grabs the hooded towel with the same hand that holds her slippery daughter. Yanking out the rubber plug, she then wrangles her son from the emptying bath because she can't turn her back on a baby in the tub. She somehow lifts him too while setting the baby down on the bathmat, their shrieking loud against the bathroom tile. Eliza takes up the moisturizer and the Caldesene powder, two diapers, and the Desitin before kneeling down and getting to work.

Amy R. and her husband, Brian, were entirely satisfied. Their first child, a sassy, dark-eyed girl, had arrived in 1999. A neat two years later, a sweet baby boy rounded out their perfect family.

Amy was tempted to have an elaborate celebration upon the giving away of the godawful maternity clothes that reminded her of feeling sick and heavy and slow for ten months at a time. She settled, instead, for a glass of wine with Brian. She felt the desire for another celebration after giving away the infant car seat when eight-month-old Miles hit twenty pounds, but had to settle for dinner out with her husband.

When an unrelated party arose—complete with well-missed college friends and fancy catering and a bartender in a pretty house in La Jolla—Amy looked upon the evening as the fête she and Brian deserved for being "done."

The long-lost friends, the plentiful cocktails from the flirtatious bartender, the fact that Brian was wearing a particularly handsome new dress shirt . . . all of this conspired with the crucial and undetectable fact that Amy happened to be ovulating. Fairly dragging Brian from a small circle of his friends, Amy led her husband, stopping mid-foyer to kiss him on the mouth and grab his package, to the office near the front hall. Conveniently, the office had a large closet into which Amy and Brian stole. Up against shelves of filing boxes holding their hosts' tax returns from the previous seven years, the Rutherfords fucked.

Amy was sure, through her Cosmopolitan haze, that this was a safe time. She had been nursing Miles and had pretty much just finished her period. Plus, just after Amy climaxed—fingertips not tarrying long what with the excitement of the party and the closet—she murmured something about pulling out. Which Brian did.

No quick withdrawal, though, could prevent the teeny swimmers in the prepuce from making their way well into Amy's choach (as the Rutherfords refer to her vagina). Propelled handily by the orgasmic contractions of the uterus, the sperm squiggled up and up, one beginning the process of penetrating its larger, rounder counterpart even as Amy pulled down her slim new-for-the-party skirt. Brian turned his sexy wife to him and kissed her once more before the happy couple exited the office and returned to the party.

———

Then there's Laura F., who claims that she and her husband, David's, success with the withdrawal method (sex approximately thrice weekly over a period of about two years) is due to the simple fact that "We're better at it than most people."

Jen W. had renovated a wonderful old house in Wellesley, Massachussetts. Jen loved her husband, Pete, who had grown up nearby in Andover. Jen and Pete had two children, which felt perfect.

Then Jen was suddenly pregnant with a third child, which was a shock. As with many surprises (most of them less momentous), Jen heeded the urge to call her trusted friend. Louise lived around the corner and happened to be an obstetrician. What was Louise's response to Jen's news that she was pregnant for a third time? That Louise was pregnant for a third time too! Jen and Louise were old friends. Their husbands were old friends. It was no coincidence that the two families had lived around the corner from each other for close to a decade. It seemed meaningful that they had been pregnant at the same time with their eldest children as well and that their children were the best of friends. With Louise's news and the enthusiasm of her husband—Pete was thrilled—Jen felt she could handle this surprise third.

The baby arrived and even with three small children at home, Jen thrived in her four-days-a-week work environment in client services for a local wealth management company.

She was content with her job and her children. She reveled in weekend trips with her brood into Cambridge or to Plum Island or Nantucket. Of course she had to sacrifice more ambitious leisure travel and there were far fewer nights out with Pete. She had less time for the running that she loved because Jen was the type of mother who spent ample one-on-one time with each child. The minivan was always cluttered. Jen missed sleeping in and reading and seeing the occasional movie. There were enough days when she felt exhausted by work and her three kids that she decided to get herself an IUD. Still, Jen experienced a kind of bliss when her three little ones filed through the door of a local restaurant or into friends' backyards or up the steps to the church she found peace in attending each Sunday.

In June 2000 Jen and her husband make their annual trip alone to New York. The swish hotel felt decadent and Jen loved the excitement that only Manhattan offers. And yet, while dining at Babbo (having had an extravagant dinner the night before at the Gotham Bar and Grill and a more casual but also delicious lunch at Pastis that noon) Jen is awash in confusion. She cannot understand why the exceptional food and wonderful atmosphere aren't making her feel good. Jen is, in fact, feeling badly. She is exhausted even far away from her three children (aged two, five, and seven). She lacks any kind of appetite and is even feeling, she tells a concerned Pete, strangely sick to her stomach. As the words cross the table Jen considers the incredible possibility—she has an IUD!—that she might be pregnant.

An EPT from a CVS confirms the unlikelihood. A second EPT confirms the first: She is pregnant. It just couldn't be, she thinks. Or could it? The possibility settles. By the following afternoon, Pete and Jen have commenced weighty deliberation.

She listens sympathetically on the bench in Washington Square as her husband tells her what she already knows: He doesn't feel strongly enough to proclaim himself pro-life or anything, but the idea of aborting a child of theirs is something he is squarely against. Jen pauses, her gaze steadily engaged with her husband's. She tells him that she knows this is difficult.

She then tells him that this has to be her decision.

If she were to have a baby for Pete she might feel terrible resentment.

If she were to have a baby against her will it might be a terrible compromise that would cause regret and distress and bitterness.

Jen loves her children deeply, unequivocally. She takes parenting very seriously. She hadn't planned on a third child. She really does not want a fourth.

On their last day in town she finds herself buoyed by long-standing plans for dinner out with her close friend Clay, who happens to have six young children. She has no plans to tell Clay about the unconfirmed pregnancy but hopes that something just might become clear in the course of the evening. The restaurant is lovely. Clay is happy and engaging and Jen actually feels better—physically—for having risen to the occasion. There are, however, several decisive moments when Jen stares at Clay, who laughs with Pete (Clay's wife is ominously not present; one of the six children is sick). Jen finds herself marveling at the fact that Clay could sit there so happily, laughing with them while six children await him at home.

Gazing earnestly out the airplane window, feeling like she is sinking, Jen turns to Pete. She tells him once more that the four days she works each week make her feel productive and appreciated. Her job proves that her brain is functioning. Working means that her expensive and hard-won education isn't for naught. She likes putting a little money in the bank.

Their house, Jen tells him, is made for three kids, not four. Her job works well with three kids. It won't with four.

Feeling defeated and sad and desperate, she reclines. She tries to nap but instead she thinks, I can't do this. I cannot handle another child. Jen had been unsure until just before she became pregnant with her first child at thirty-two that she ever wanted to have children at all. She readjusts the little airplane pillow and reminds herself that her mother survived five children. Jen was the eldest of five children. But maybe her mother had been right when she once said that Jen was ambivalent about having children because she had mothered so many younger siblings.

The flight attendants make their way through the cabin picking up the last of the trash and Jen considers how overwhelmed she sometimes feels by her three young kids. Raising them well is harder than any corporate demands she has ever met. Their needs seem to be growing and Jen's expectations of herself are rising accordingly. She is becoming further convinced—as the turbulence of their descent exacerbates her nausea and makes her appreciate, for the first time, the presence of air-sickness bags—that she would not be a good mother if she had four children.

Outside in the soothing chill at Logan, though, Jen's quantitative mind fixes on probability. She is moved as she says to Pete, the numbers seeming even weightier as she speaks them in the parking garage, that the odds of having conceived this baby were less than one in a hundred.

They pull up to the house. Pete settles up with the babysitter while Jen takes the time to reestablish soothing, sincere, individual contact with each of her children. She kisses Pete and thanks him for the wonderful weekend before piling the kids into the minivan, her exhaustion making Louise's house around the corner seem far too far to walk.

At her best friend's kitchen table, Jen shares her soft-spoken news and is disappointed by the predictable response that Louise—with whom she has shared uncanny reproductive timing—is not in fact pregnant for a fourth time. But Jen has come around the corner for more than the comforting ear of a friend. Jen asks obstetrician Louise about abortion and her friend walks her through the procedure.

The idea of terminating the pregnancy leads Jen and Pete to their pastor. Jen smiles about this later, conceding that a meeting with your pastor to discuss abortion sounds kind of strange. Maybe Jen was indulging her husband's interests. Maybe it was her moral conflict and heightened emotion. The pastor Jen and Pete saw—in a small room during a difficult hour stolen from a busy schedule—is a young, judicious woman. This pastor speaks of God having given Jen an opportunity. The pastor says that Jen will not be doing this alone. God will give her strength.

The amazing thing is that Jen, who was fairly sure she would have an abortion, was swayed. At select points in her life religion has proved a guiding force or consolation, but she does not consider herself an overly religious person. She has always wanted to share the ardent faith that her parents and siblings prize but hasn't always felt it. There in the pastor's office she is struck by the phrase "change of heart." She will later use the words "by the grace of God." It is the sanctified hour with the pastor that leads Jen to accept this fourth child.

Back at home, in the rhythm of her children, this pregnancy begins to feel . . . extraordinary. Jen knows this sounds a little outlandish. Still, the idea of a child growing inside of her body despite the presence of birth control is astounding. Jen is filled with conviction that this pregnancy is God's way of bringing her closer to Him, something she has been wanting. This pregnancy—she tells Pete as they finally crawl into bed a few nights later—feels miraculous.

Young Oliver is born and Jen expects him to pop out with the duplicitous IUD in hand (no one has seen it in ultrasounds but apparently the fetus can obstruct the view), but her fourth child is accompanied by no hardware. This prompts doctors to conclude that at some point before his conception Jen had expelled the device.

Laughing softly at the idea of having expelled something like that without knowing it, Jen jokes (serenely, mildly) that maybe Oliver wasn't the miracle baby she had assumed he was, then reiterates that of course she still believes this child is miraculous. Every day Jen looks at young Oliver and wonders what his purpose is. She watches as he dances or wails and throws himself floorward or jumps on the trampoline outside her playroom window and Jen considers whether he is, today, making her a better person.

Jen remembers no disbelief, no skepticism at the doctors' claim that she had passed a three-inch T-shaped piece of copper through her undilated cervix and out of her vagina. Who has time for conjecture when there are four young children at home and work is a thing of the past and your days are incomparably full (or empty)?

She remembers no skepticism even on the night when she woke screaming with acute abdominal pain (Louise receiving a frightened phone call from Pete, Louise rushing around the corner in her pajamas to say that she can offer no real diagnosis but she can, at least, of course! stay with the four sleeping kids). No one even doubted the emergency room doctors early the next morning—least of all Jen who was in the euphoric wake that follows acute pain—when they diagnosed acid reflux for what had been reported as severe pain in the pelvic region.

The mystery of the IUD would go unsolved, forgotten really, until just after young Oliver's first birthday, and after a two-hundred-mile running relay race from Killington to Boston that Jen, who had played competitive squash at school, had just finished running with a group of friends. At home the morning after the race, with the insistent three-year-old at her side and young Oliver (who has an earache) crying in the playroom, Jen hurries in the bathroom as mothers must. She finishes her business and rises from the toilet.

She might not have seen it, the mystery might have gone completely unresolved because of the way Oliver's crying was ratcheting up and her eldest son was calling, "Mommy!" But in the quickest of glances, Jen sees in the smallish poop there in the toilet bowl, the shining copper T.

Her laughter, a burst of it, startles the three-year-old. Jen is aghast. She gapes. This can't be! This means that her IUD has traveled through organs and tissue and bowel walls. After leaving the bathroom, gathering up crying Oliver and answering her eldest son's question, Jen calls Louise. She asks if it's medically possible to expel an IUD . . . in this way. She says "bowel movement" then "poop" and "even the little string-thing and everything."

In her own kitchen with her three young kids, Louise is astounded right along with Jen. Louise laughs. Louise says that never in the history of obstetrics has she heard of such a thing. She says Jen should head straight over to Brigham and Womens' because they are absolutely going to want to write this up (which Jen eventually does, and they eventually do).

While Louise delves into further medical unlikelihood, what Jen feels is a kind of strength. She is thinking that her body must be uncommonly strong. It's amazing she didn't have some kind of infection. Or a lot more pain. Her body had produced and carried and given birth to four children. She had just run almost twenty miles. For years she has functioned perfectly well while a foreign object made its way through her abdomen.

She thinks of how she'll be a little embarrassed to tell Pete that she pooped out her IUD. She says to Louise, "Wait 'til Pete hears I pooped out my IUD."

Jen sighs then and mentions the long night with earachy Oliver. They talk about what they had for breakfast and Louise tells Jen about a delicious new kind of Greek yogurt. Then Louise's middle son needs her and Jen's five-year-old needs her. They remark again how strange this IUD situation is, after which Jen and Louise make a plan to meet, with their seven kids between them, at the park.

————

On a Tuesday in the spring of 1998, Nikki D. buckled her three unwieldy children into the car seats of her sour-milk-scented Town and Country. Once down at her friend Kim's, she hustled up the stone path with the one-year-old on her hip, the two-year-old's sticky hand in hers, three-year-old Adam blazing an erratic trail through the garden. Yanking on the two-year-old's hand, Nikki tried to keep up as Adam rounded the corner of the tiny house and barreled through a front door that slammed against its wall, making his mother not so much jump as cringe.

There on the couch, looking a little agog at the explosion of energy into her calm little house, sat Kim. Kim (appearing perhaps a tad critical) was reading a thousand-page edition of *À la recherche du temps perdu* that, in Nikki's opinion, looked totally and completely boring. Kim, who had known Nikki since high school, sat not only with her book but also with a cup of perfectly steeped tea that she rested on her pregnant belly. Staring at Nikki and her children, Kim managed to look both tranquil and totally put-upon, as only women pregnant with their first child can manage to appear.

Nikki slid tiny Julia to the floor. She rifled through her enormous bulging Pierre Deux diaper bag. "Oh my God, am I glad you're here. I need you to pee on something."

Kim hadn't even managed "what?" (so intently was she watching Adam pull her precious nineteenth-century French and Spanish tomes off the low shelf and onto the floor) before Nikki whipped out one of the half-dozen EPT's—Ed and Nikki, Catholics, were practicing the "Rhythm Method"— that Nikki kept under the bathroom sink next to an impressive array of many-sized diapers.

Nikki thrust the box at Kim while reaching down to scoop up now howling Julia who had just smacked her little round head on the big, square non-baby-proofed coffee table.

With one hand on her round belly, the other holding the EPT, Kim said, "I'm already pretty sure I'm pregnant."

"No, no." Nikki set Julia down with a brisk pat on her teeny saggy-diapered bottom. "It's not for you. It's for me. Well, for Ed, really. Today is April Fools'!"

Now, in Kimberly's serious graduate school reality, April 1 meant only that her exams were one day closer than they had been on March 31.

For Nikki, whose life consisted of equal parts tedium and chaos, April Fools' Day provided important deviation from the lackluster norm. Nikki lived for this stuff. After Ed had risen from the table at a New Year's Eve celebration the year before and publicly resolved not to get his wife pregnant in 1997, as he had in '95 and '96, Nikki actually broke the exciting news of her third pregnancy with a quip in a local newspaper some months later. "Have you kept your New Year's resolution?" the announcement read. "Edward Duane hasn't!"

Pleased enough to be involved in one of Nikki's pranks (not knowing Ed quite well enough to anticipate his desire for revenge), Kim peed on the little stick. She then offered to make tea for Nikki, who gulped half of it down before having to carry through on the threat that they would leave "right this minute!" if middle-child Alex couldn't quit chasing the cranky dog around the dining-room table.

That evening, their three children finally in bed for the first sleep stint of the night, Nikki stood next to Ed at the double sinks in their bathroom. As her husband finished brushing his teeth, Nikki said, "I have a surprise for you."

From her mischievous smile Ed assumed she meant sex, his dick coming to attention as he rinsed and faced her with, "What?"

From the pocket of her silk robe came the white plastic EPT.

Never had an erection disappeared so instantly.

Ed stared at the dark purple lines as though they were drafting him into a foreign war or proclaiming a fatal diagnosis. He did not look up at Nikki. He did not laugh or hug her or weep tears of joy. He lowered his head further.

"April Fools'!" yelled his wife.

He looked up with disbelief. "This is a joke?" He looked back at the EPT. "This is *not* funny."

"It's April Fools'. It's a joke!" But Nikki was experiencing that sinking feeling in her stomach when she had really fucked something up.

Nikki was saddened and surprised because it had looked for a minute like Ed was going to say she needed an abortion. Nikki would never, ever have thought of having an abortion because her parents had each died in the past four years. Nikki and Ed had moved to Montclair to be close to her parents through their illnesses and it had been awful. Sure her kids were a little wild and of course she was overwhelmed sometimes, but Nikki thrived on chaos. She was intent upon filling her days (not to mention the house that now teemed with her parents' furniture and their books and their grand piano) with life. More children meant more life around her and Nikki had felt a distinct pang of loss at seeing her pregnant friend that afternoon and realizing that she might never again feel a baby moving inside of her. Nikki had often—not so much in her husband's company— toyed with the idea of a fourth.

Ed had once lamented only half-teasingly that unlike writer Ayelet Waldman, who had caused a media storm when she claimed that she might consider choosing her husband over her four children if faced with the proverbial life raft, Nikki would toss her husband overboard without a second thought. There in the bathroom, Ed looked pained. His expression made him seem a decade older than his thirty-three years and Nikki would later say that her prank may have taken that many years off his life. "This," he said, "is not a good joke. This isn't funny."

She was disappointed that her husband hadn't welcomed the idea of another child, but mostly Nikki was worried because he looked so injured. She wanted to pull herself to him but she felt too repentant. In a voice meant to convey contrition she said, "I'm sorry. I thought it would be funny." Looking sheepishly at him, trying to engage her husband and make the whole thing better, she quietly repeated, "April Fools'!"

———

Kendall N. and her husband were fucking. They were fucking in the hip, if tiny, loft that they both loved in the East Village. They were fucking just after their delightfully easy three-year-old, Thayer, had fallen asleep in his perfect little alcove of a room off the adult sleeping space in the loft's upper reaches. Kendall, somewhat surprisingly, had been the one to initiate sex that evening. She herself had been a little amazed by having spent the day (at work at the Putnam Gallery) thinking not of the abstract art she loved or of the monthlong trip to France their perfect family was about to take, but of sex.

Which should have been a sign.

Kendall could not get little Thayer into bed early enough. Kendall couldn't remember the last time she had hurried quite so much when ripping the little foil packet and unrolling the condom onto her husband's penis. Kendall couldn't remember sex feeling so good.

Which was, in part, because when Kendall had hurriedly unrolled the condom onto her husband's very erect member she had pressed down a little too hard. The minute Rob thrust his dick into her the rubber snapped.

(Kendall would be shocked, six weeks later in their sleek bathroom with its white subway tile. She and Rob had been adamant about only one child. Their lives were perfect with just little Thayer. Kendall had said to more than one girl-friend, "If I ever got pregnant again I would absolutely have to shoot myself." Yet six weeks later Kendall would stare down at the two dark lines on the EPT and would register what could only be called—impractical, illogical, utterly unforeseen—elation.)

But for now Kendall N. was lost in sensation. In the energy concentrating at her center, in the uncommon richness of her husband's (unsheathed) cock inside of her. As she rubbed her clit hard against her husband's abdomen, the waves of sensation mounted and mounted to break over and through her.

Kendall called out so loudly that Thayer—the perfect only child in his perfect IKEA bed in his perfect little alcove—woke up. Ever content, though, little Thayer simply kicked off his covers, rolled over, and fell back to sleep.

CHAPTER 15

Pleasure Party

Meanwhile, Sara stood in the sex section of the bookstore, thumbing through volume after volume. Nothing seemed right. No book fit how she felt. When Sara got home, she was totally fed up and depressed. Jim's excitement, however, was palpable. He showed her his new book, his favorite drawings, and the cans of whipped cream.

—John M. Gottman, Ph.D., and
Susan Schwartz Gottman, Ph.D.
And Baby Makes Three

Rebecca Brewer stands on our front porch with briefcase in hand. She's twenty-three and self-assuredly curvy under full-legged black pants and a pale smocky blouse, exuding more of a playful energy than the blatant sensuality I expected from my Good Vibrations Pleasure Party Consultant. As the kids and I welcome her into the living room Rebecca treats us to her quick laughter. Bill rises from the couch where we have been having a glass of wine. She says hello to him. She greets the dog, then each child individually. Her dark hair is pulled back in a no-nonsense ponytail that reveals her pretty face, Lucas and Hannah doing a decent job of not staring at the thickish black hoop piercing her bottom lip.

Four-year-old Xavier, on the other hand, is saucer-eyed.

Becca asks his name, but instead of offering it he says, "Does it *hurt*?"

She lowers herself instinctively to his level. "Just for a second," she says, slightly misunderstanding his question while bringing the unsettling visual closer to him. "Like a shot. Or maybe not quite so painful."

"Oh," says Xavier, and I am proud when he clarifies his original question. "But," he visibly flinches, "does it hurt right *now*?"

And we smile. She assures him it doesn't as Bill ushers the kids into the office where he plans to watch a movie with them because the shopping bag Becca has brought holds party favors that are far from child-appropriate. Not to mention the other large tote Becca fetches from the porch. I couldn't have imagined its contents had I tried.

Just then Simone and Ruby arrive, followed by Allison and Kate, Katherine, Jen, Tess, and Liz. As Becca sets up, we women move to the kitchen for glasses of wine and a small birthday cake for salt-and-pepper Allison who was born on February 29, which always leaves us nice flexibility as to which day we choose for a fête.

The women gathering around Allison's flourless chocolate decadence are largely the same ones who assembled in this house two years ago for the series of erotic dance evenings with Catherine Rose. We are mothers whose boys have moved from kindergarten to first to second then onto third grade, women whose husbands have grown accustomed to commentary about vibrators and privacy strategies and pubic hair removal while we all sit at dinner parties or celebratory evenings for each of our birthdays.

Simone mixes vodka tonics for herself and Ruby, whose hair is held back in a demure scarf that is saved from looking

schoolmarmish by its feisty golden sheen. Ruby pulls a silvery wrapped gift from her bag, having just explained that
she wore her eyeglasses especially for the Pleasure Party:
"To be able to see all this excellent shit really well."

She then spins around and engages in a jiggly kind of
ass-shaking farce of an erotic dance move that looked just a
tad better on Catherine Rose. Finishing with a flourish, she
hands our birthday girl her present. "That was 'The
Candy,'" Ruby says of her move. "This little gift is in honor
of how excellent Allison was at it."

The gift? Allison removes paper and tissue to reveal a pair
of panties made of those small pastel kiddy candies seen
most often on elastic bracelets and necklaces.

At the close of our seminal—and yes, pleasureful—
evening, Allison will shuffle out the door with the
wriggly panties on under her skirt. She will report the
next day at drop-off that they were fun. "It was a hoot!"
Allison will say before adding that John liked them a lot,
but that they were "just really sticky."

Allison thanks Ruby with a squeezy hug. "This is totally
perfect. Honestly. Timing couldn't be better for candy underwear. And you know what? I need a new vibrator. My
poor little Beefeater . . . He gave up the ghost."

Vibrators. This is the one thing we mothers expect from
the evening though none of us has ever attended a sex toy
party. We assume there will be laughter and blushing and
the empowering kind of embarrassment that comes from
gangs of mothers getting in touch with their libidos. But
even before we head into the living room I sense a mature
composure that differs from the silly, more inebriated aban-

don that was required to bust a "Butt Show" or try "The Nasty" with Catherine Rose. We mothers have graduated from erotic dance but I like to think that our talented instructor would be pleased at the open discussions of sex and vibrators and orgasms that are the legacy of her workshops.

The overriding emotion, though, as we move into this next sexy adventure feels markedly different from the amped-up camaraderie generated at erotic dance. "Pleasure Party" is marked by collective curiosity, by a more serious desire for knowledge, which I appreciate. As we leave the kitchen, I grab a bottle of wine because there have been jokes about needing a drink or three. The wine will go largely untouched as we ladies experience the unexpected.

We love Becca immediately because of how she makes eye contact and smiles and says "hi" and "hello" in an affable yet composed and good-natured way as we file in. We gather around the oval coffee table, seating ourselves on the couch and armchairs and little stools, Becca standing before the large front window. As I settle in I understand that her appeal lies partly in the maternal air (despite being twenty-three) of her soothing voice, in her rounded arms and large breasts, in the way she seems genuinely engaged with us as a group before she even introduces herself.

We like Becca because she graduated from the University of California at Berkeley in 2005 with a BA in "Sexuality: An Interdisciplinary Look," a major that she herself created and that Berkeley, being Berkeley, accepted. How could we not love a woman whose senior thesis was called "Giving Lip Service: Female Masturbation, Erotica and the Freudian Legacy"?

Becca completes her brief description of herself with the fact that she has "a strong commitment to sex positivity."

She works not only as a Good Vibrations Pleasure Party Consultant but also full-time at the Daly City Youth Health Center and also at the Center for Sex & Culture where she is an off-site educator currently giving a course called "Reclaiming Masturbation." When this garners perplexed expressions from us mothers, Becca explains that the class is intended for college-age kids, to which we say, "ohhhh," each mother hoping her child's one-day orgasm won't need reclaiming.

"I like to begin each evening," Becca continues, "with some words about Good Vibrations," because she is indeed representing the legendary Northern California sex shop. "Good Vibrations was founded in 1977 by Joani Blank, who was doing extensive work at the time with pre-orgasmic women."

"Now right." Ruby pushes her glasses up her nose. "Kim and I were just talking about this. I mean—is it okay to interrupt?"

Becca nods encouragingly.

"We were just wondering yesterday about those women we used to know who had never had an orgasm. That is just so sad. There must still be women out there who don't have orgasms. Or not?"

"Sure." Becca is clearly inspired by Ruby's concern. "The pre-orgasmic women Joani Blank worked with were between the ages of eighteen and seventy. So yeah, there are plenty of women out there who need guidance to achieve their potential."

"Right." Ruby nods empathetically.

"So what did Joani recommend? Her feeling was that each of these women would really benefit from a vibrator. In 1977, buying a vibrator wasn't usually a positive experience. The

shops were hard to find. They were sometimes dirty or otherwise unpleasant. The vibrators might be up on the high-
est shelves. The men would call them sluts."

"Nooo," and "Oohh," we lament.

"Yes," confirms Becca. "Joani felt there was a need and
Good Vibrations came into being." (In fact, here's Joani
Blank's mission-type statement from the excellent *Good Vibrations Guide to Sex*: "There is a great deal more sexual pleasure available than most of us experience, and getting it
need not be difficult, expensive, or dangerous" [8].)

With a theatrical air born of conviction and enthusiasm
Rebecca then turns to the antique melodeon, a fancy old-
school piano that mostly looks like a sideboard, behind her.
This pretty piece of furniture belonged to my father's
mother, a woman we called Granny, its sheeny cherry surface now mounded with Becca's fascinating wares.

She turns back, though, not with the enormous rubber
dildo I expect, but with an unidentifiable pillowlike item
some twelve inches tall.

"This." Becca announces, "Is our Wondrous Vulva
Puppet!"

The satiny cream-colored longitudinal folds along its
sides suddenly do look like labia. I see the reddish folds inside the outer ones and am pleased to recognize the inner
labia. I am especially proud to identify the sharpei-like folds
of scarlet cloth at the top of the thing as the clitoral hood.

"I like this plush labia for a lot of reasons," our trusty
leader begins.

Ruby can't resist. "Talk about a lovey!" She then imitates
any mother. "Having a hard time sleeping, Baby? Here. Take
your plush labia." She leaves off, turning to me. "Maybe
that's what Kim needed!" she says, referring to my extensive

efforts with blankie after stuffy after binky—all of which my children flatly refused in favor of near-constant nursing.

Pausing patiently, seemingly content at our animation, Becca then says, "One of the things I like very best about this plush labia is right here." She points to a slight bulge at the lower part of the right inner labia.

"Asymmetry." Becca beams. "It's very important to remember that each vulva is like a face." She then shuttles us back to Good Vibrations' founding decade: "Every vulva is different, every vulva is beautiful.

"It's important to be sure that a woman has a good understanding of pleasure physiology." She smiles and lowers her voice as though imparting a secret. "Pleasure physiology is my favorite part of my job." Then Becca continues, picking up speed as she reviews what she assumes is common knowledge, though I want her to slow down because this rush of anatomical terms is so good to hear out loud. I'm pleased when Ruby cries, "Wait! Go slower!"

"Oh, okay, yeah," says Becca, who is clearly very excited about all the information she has to impart in the mere two hours we busy mothers can spare on a school night. "These larger folds here are the outer labia. These will be covered with coarse hair. If they aren't, some kind of depilation has taken place."

At which Allison cries, "Ah-hah!" and points an accusing finger across the circle to where Ruby lounges on the big couch and I sit on my little stool. Ruby is unafraid, though, to fire back collegially that Allison's depilation style (John shaving her on that towel) is a little racier than the laser hair removal (see "Laser Lover") the two of us have gone in for.

Again Becca gamely indulges our banter before returning to business: "Here we have the inner labia. And this is the urethra." She points to a spot I can't see in the upper third of the center of the pillow and I swear I'm not the only one to wince at that aspect of the female genital design. "Up here is the clitoral hood," which Becca pulls back, "and this . . ." she slows, her features softening reverentially. "This is the clitoris.

"You have to love," Becca says, "your clit." She grins. "I've been dying to make a T-shirt that reads LOVE YOUR CLIT. You just have to love it because the clitoris is the key to any orgasm."

And though this is not entirely new to us, we are rapt.

"But we might be getting ahead of ourselves," corrects Becca. "Who can tell me the first erogenous zone to be engaged?"

I find it impossible to think (narrow-mindedly) beyond the clitoris as Ruby yells, "Your mind!"

To which Becca says, "Yes."

"When your brain becomes engaged erotically," she informs us, "you experience 'sex flush.' This is the redirection of blood from organs to your skin and other principal erogenous zones. The basic equation I like to use is: blood flow + nerve endings = arousal.

"Areas with many nerve endings respond well to more subtle stimulation such as licking, sucking, stroking, tugging, and vibration." (This magical series will be repeated so often in the course of the evening that Ruby soon suggests we come up with an acronym. Becca gladly accepts the challenge, but to her LSSTV sounds "like some kind of drug," which then makes her laugh because "sex really can be," she opines, "better than the best of drugs.")

"That kind of marked response to stimuli," Becca continues, "is why we all really need to love our clits."

"But," asks Simone, who reportedly—along with Katherine—has an orgasm if her husband so much as glances in her direction, "what about the vaginal orgasm? What's that all about?"

"Excellent question," Becca says. "To answer that we need to understand the anatomy of the clitoris." She holds up the plush labia. "The clitoris is shaped just like a wishbone: The 'head' is here." She points to the protuberance of fabric under the pulled-back hood. "Now imagine a 'shaft' reaching back into the body an inch or an inch and a half. 'Legs' then come down on either side of the vagina—parallel to the labia . . . here and here . . . and are approximately three inches in length. Women who experience what they refer to as 'vaginal orgasm,' are usually perceiving stimulation of the clitoral legs."

At which point I look to Jen and Kate who are seated to my left. With genuine wonder I say, "Who knew?"

And I mean this as more than a cute response. I turn to Katherine, the MD on my right, who is sitting next to Tess, an MD so prominent in the field of obstetrics that she gives courses at Stanford (Tess is a personal favorite of mine because she brought the pair of amazingly comfortable Hanky Panky underwear I ended up with when we held an accessory exchange at one of the erotic dance class nights.) "Seriously," I ask our two medical professionals. "Did you guys know that?"

Tess's eyes widen. "New to me."

Katherine looks back to Becca as if my question is a waste of our precious time. "Pleasure physiology? Not a priority in any med school I know of."

Becca seems happy with our enlightenment but totally unsurprised at the medical community's disinterest in her specialization. You can tell from the way she's swaying side to side (again giving her a maternal air, her motion that of new parents who tend to sway even without the tiny babe in their arms) that Becca is eager to move on to an even more detailed description of the clitoris. Some of this isn't new to us. Like the fact that the clitoris is more sensitive than the penis. What none among us could quantify, however, is that the clitoris is made up of over eight thousand nerve bundles, more than twice the number in the entire penis.

"All concentrated in such a tiny space," marvels Simone, nodding as if finally understanding her orgasmic ease.

"Exactly," says Becca. "One thing to consider is that all those concentrated nerves can make for overstimulation," which gets nods from other women in the room. We are moderately surprised by Becca's report that approximately only 10 percent of women report "vaginal orgasm." Surprise increases when we learn that Freud was the one who created the myth. Becca, clearly not a devotee of the father of psychoanalysis, explains rather dismissively that Freud considered the "vaginal orgasm" a superior, more evolved form of pleasure because the clitoris is nothing more than a small penis, clitoral orgasm thus being nothing more than a negligible manifestation of penis envy.

Also left untouched by most med schools, most Sex Ed programs and the majority of edifying conversations among young women is Becca's next physiological revelation.

"Now, my plush labia can do something most vaginas can't." To demonstrate her next surprise she turns the scarlet socklike vagina inside out. Ever the annoying teacher's pet, I call out, "Prolapse! Prolapse!" having learned the term from my nurse friend Heather at our co-op preschool.

"Yes," Becca indulges me, though this isn't what she's eager to show us. "It is prolapsed."

What she wants us to see is a light yellow strip of material running up the inner-upper wall of the vagina. "Can anyone tell me what this is?"

Ruby guesses pee, then giggles.

"This is the peri-urethral sponge." When Becca fails to receive the recognition she expected she says, "The G-spot!"

"No" and "Oh!" and "I thought the G-spot was a myth," we call out.

"Far from it," insists Becca, making me wonder how a group of women as well-educated as we are (nearly every one of us holds an advanced degree of some sort) could be so woefully undereducated in the mechanics of pleasure.

(Turns out that the peri-urethral sponge—according to the *GV Guide to Sex*—"is what has come to be called the G-spot . . . named for Ernst Grafenberg, a gynecologist who first published research on the erotic pleasure potential of the urethra in the 1940s and 1950s. Some women greatly enjoy stimulating the urethral sponge, and some women experience an ejaculation of fluids through the urethra as a result" [19].)

"If," continues Becca, "you're curious about reaching your female ejaculatory potential" . . . and just as I'm thinking how funny "female ejaculatory potential" sounds, Allison shouts, "*That's* what that was!!"

Over our laughter Allison cries, "It was the craziest thing! I'm not kidding. I'm really glad to know this. It only happened this one time. When we were first dating. It was," she laughs so hard she cannot speak, then finally manages, "this gush!"

"Uh-huh," says Becca, smiling, and goes on to impress us

all with the fact that this fluid may come out of the urethra but that it isn't at all like urine. It is instead, "very close in chemical makeup to semen, but without the sperm!"

"Unbelievable," remarks a satisfied Allison. "I have always just thought, what the hell was that?! Now I know."

The rest of us are further impressed at the idea that Allison may well have done exactly what Becca then recommends for any of us who might be "curious about attaining our ejaculatory potential": First, have several clitoral orgasms (Becca says this as though having "several clitoral orgasms" is effortless, which seems absurd only because haven't we heard the rest of her presentation); then stimulate the G-Spot.

"Like this," she says. She raises her hand. "Your partner can use one, or two—even three fingers if you're feeling particularly saucy." She then moves a pair of fingers in a simple come hither way, her palm facing the ceiling to stimulate the front wall of the vagina and I swear one among us draws a small diagram of Becca's hand on her catalog.

"But go back to 'several clitoral orgasms,'" says Kate.

"Sure." And Becca—lo and behold—raises my beloved Magic Wand.

"Shoot." Tess is agog at the enormous breadth, the medical-grade white plastic, and the lengthy electrical cord dangling from the sixteen-inch vibrator. "It'd be like having another person in bed with you."

But on I smile. As Becca begins to extol my preferred tool's virtues, I can't resist interjecting my own little statistic: "Four excellent orgasms in twelve minutes! The first time I plugged it in!" which ratio results in Liz dogearing the catalog page where my Wand poses magisterially among multicolored neoprene and silicone and rubber accoutrements. The thing looks so durable and timeless that Simone, whose widowed mother is seventy-three, calls out, "I'll get one for my mom, and one day . . . it'll be mine!" Simone, Kate, Liz, and I then decide the moment has arrived to present Allison with her very own birthday Magic Wand. Allison cradles the large box, looking honored and pleased that her little Beefeater is being replaced with something so fabulous.

Not until our birthday girl writes Kate a formal thank-you note on monogrammed Crane's stationery will Allison confide, "I have to admit I was worried the Wand would be too big—but NO!" (Kate herself admits to loving the irony of receiving such a formal note—more and more rare in this relaxed, electronic age—as thanks for a vibrator.)

We then refocus. I'm busy putting "reach ejaculatory potential" on my mental "List of Goals to Achieve" while Becca moves from demonstration of this nonpareil vibrator to more anatomy, male this time. The taupe-colored rubber penis she holds up before us isn't half as charming as the vulva puppet, a fact that Becca acknowledges. "We would love a plush penis. We've had a few prototypes. They keep falling apart."

First she touches on the more sensitive parts of the penis, beginning with the glans, or the head. (Allison asks about differences between circumcised and uncircumcised, the latter, it turns out, being more sensitive—overly sensitive in some cases). Becca spends a little time on the seam running along the underside of the penis, then the perineum; she speaks of the pleasure capacity of the anus, promising—as some of us noticeably squirm—that we will come back to that. Becca then moves on to the real shocker: the prostate.

"Best-known for cancer," she remarks as though reading my mind, "the prostate is actually analogous to the peri-urethral sponge."

There is a collective gasp.

"The G-spot," Becca confirms, "is analogous to the P-spot!"

Again I am surprised. "Who knew?"

"Mmm-hmm," Becca nods. "Many men report amazingly enhanced orgasms while experiencing prostate massage. Some men can take it or leave it, but many *really* enjoy this kind of stimulation."

"Wait." Ruby whips off her glasses and scoots to the edge of the couch. "This is me . . . sticking my finger up my husband's butt?"

"Yes," says Becca. "I know. We all have a lot of butt taboos."

"It's just . . ." Allison is laughing her silent, shaking laughter again, "It's just . . . the poop. It wouldn't be so bad . . ."

"Yeah," joins Liz, "if it weren't for poop!"

"Don't get me wrong," Ruby clarifies, "you all know how much I love my husband. I'm just not sure I want to stick my finger up his ass."

As if to give us time to process the idea, Becca busies herself with the selection of something from atop Granny's melodeon. She turns back and stares out over us to impart the momentousness of the item, then raises "Aneros." Aneros is a simple piece of white plastic with a three-inch shaft about a half inch in diameter, with twin scrolls forming its slim base. Designed by doctors for prostate massage, use of the device is said to reduce the risk of cancer. It has no batteries, no motor, nothing. Becca takes up a sheet of paper and reads a few testimonials from real men who use phrases like "mind-altering," "completely unexpected," and most impressively, "over an hour of the most intense pleasure I have ever experienced." We wives shuffle through order forms and catalogs to check out the description of this small piece of plastic we are meant, unfathomably, to put up our husband's butts while having intercourse.

"You just go about sex like the thing's not even there?" cries Ruby.

"Mmm-humm," confirms Becca.

"Well, shit." She giggles. "Looks like I might have found a solution!"

————————

Though Ruby will ultimately decide against the "Aneros," at least one among us will be sufficiently daring. More than a month later I will be standing between Allison and John by the barbecue where John is basting a side of ribs.

"Oh God," Allison will blurt as though remembering something she's been meaning to tell me. Her eyes will then crinkle as she laughs the silent laughter that means she's about to say something bawdy.

"What?" I will cry.

"Things did *not*," she will finally manage, "go well with the butt plug."

"What butt plug?" I search recent memory, then seize upon it. "The Aneros?!"

"Is that what it was called?" Allison will ask, the name sending her into more silent paroxysms.

John will shake his head while smiling adoringly at his wife.

"Did you not read the testimonials?" I'll ask. "I mean,

my God, those testimonials! And Becca said it helps prevent prostate cancer. The thing's a medical device!"

Allison will pull herself together enough to say, "We only got to the part where they recommend . . ." again she'll dissolve into shaking laughter.

I will chuckle myself.

"We just couldn't get beyond," a smiling John will finish for his weeping wife, "the part in the instructions where they recommend you 'rest for fifteen minutes after insertion into the anus.'"

From the P-spot Becca moves us on to the multitude of vibrators we have been expecting but are wowed by nonetheless. Around our small circle travel vibes that Becca suggests we test with the tip of our noses though not one of us does because simply holding these items in our hands seems enough. We test the popular Turbo Glider (Blueberry or Raspberry) that Becca bills as a good "beginner's vibe." There's a hands-free model called the Femblossom that looks like a small, slightly curved white dessert plate. Ruby orders this one straight away, her plan being to sit on the thing during drives to and from the city where she takes voice lessons. Simone follows suit and buys a Femblossom for herself.

A mere four days after the Pleasure Party, our Open Enterprises packages will begin appearing on each of our doorsteps. A palpable frisson will run through our neighborhood as phone calls and murmurs of "Did you get your stuff?" make their way through town. Simone will discover her own squarish box on the front step as she enters the house behind her seventy-three-year-old mother, Annika, who will have just flown in that morning from Ohio. Some half-hour later, Simone's mother will come walking down the dim hallway to where Simone will be folding the work clothes she will have just changed out of.

ANNIKA: Simone? Dear. I have something for you.

SIMONE: [Looking up to see, there in her mother's hand, the white, plate-shaped Femblossom] Oh. Mom . . . uh . . .

ANNIKA: [Raising the shifty item toward the light where it now has a flash of silver, the Femblossom appearing to have suddenly sprouted a blade] I brought you a mushroom slicer!

Back in the living room, the assortment of vibrators seems limitless. There's the G-Swirl, the G-Twist, the Night Rider and the surprising SWAK Kit ("because it looks like a mouth—you know, Sealed With A Kiss!"), that is designed especially for men. "Because the glans," Becca reminds us, "is another nerve-ending-rich area that loves," here she pauses, indulging Ruby's earlier suggestion, trying this time to pronounce the acronym, "LuhSSTuhV" then smiling and simply reeling off "licking, stroking, sucking, tugging, and vibration." The unusual SWAK Kit is followed by the plethora of Rabbits and their derivatives, then waterproof vibrators, then vinyl and elastomer and bullet vibes. Becca is forthcoming about these products, explaining which are manufactured by the German medical device company that places a premium on quality but can be pricey. She tells us which vibes are not as durable, which are more intense, which are nearly silent, and which can be really, really loud.

Catholic Liz will wait until the afternoon of her six-teenth wedding anniversary to unpack her smallish Open Enterprises box. Liz will be reluctant. Liz is not a sex toy person. She will peer into the box the afternoon it arrives, see little more than packing peanuts, and shut it again. She will hide it under her bed so neither her four kids nor the babysitter will ever discover its sure-to-be mortifying contents.

Liz and her husband, Jack, will have celebrated their anniversary with dinner out at fancy Marché during which each will have had a vodka tonic and several glasses of pinot noir. After returning home and paying the babysitter, Jack and Liz will retire to the bedroom. Only after the lights are well dimmed will inebriated Liz summon the great courage necessary to reach under the bed. She will fumble with the box and extract the Lady Luster. She will be looking down so intently at the translucent purple vibrator (trying to figure out how to make it go) that she will miss the unprecedented excitement in her husband's Irish Catholic face.

More fumbling. Liz will twist some purple part or another. The room will then fill with a roar that threatens to instantly wake all four children. The vibrator sounds like a lawnmower. Like a helicopter! Liz will not know what to do. She will turn it and twist it but the Lady Luster will not stop. Liz, who played competitive volleyball at the boarding school she attended in Santa Barbara, will chuck the thing across the room. The poor device will clunk against the wall and thump to the floor, where it will fall silent.

And not only vibrators! Becca shows us strap-ons, one called the Bend Over Boyfriend, about which I have to inquire, feeling naïve when Becca says, "You wear this. Your boyfriend bends over and you penetrate." These strap-ons are meant to be coupled with dildos whose Western names—Outlaw, Bandit, Lonestar—lead me to imagine otherwise conservative Texans trafficking in a lot of "harnessable" sex toys.

The evening after the Pleasure Party my mom will stop by for a postprandial cup of tea. She will leaf through the *GV* catalog sitting on the kitchen counter. She will hope to get a rise out of Bill by pointing to the Strap It To Me Kit.

"Is this a good one, Bill? Should I order this one?"

Clever Bill (who hasn't had any experience with strap-ons that I know of) comes right back with, "Nah, I wouldn't go with that one. Slips around a lot."

After the strap-ons come the dildos. A particularly rubbery one with a powerful suction-cup base looks especially odd when Becca merrily whaps it onto the side of Granny's melodeon to suggest how effectively suction toys might be used in the shower or on your headboard. "Or at the kitchen sink!" cries Liz, who is a professionally trained chef.

Butt plugs and beads lead to more dialogue about anal taboos. And boy do I really have to hand it to Becca with her forthright, positive description of how to make anal sex work. The three important rules are: 1. LOTS and LOTS of lube. 2. Take it slow. 3. Always have a base on anything you use for anal penetration! She actually succeeds in making a previously divisive and squirmy topic feel like yet another adventure each of us should consider. It's her affable, straightforward approach that creates the atmosphere in which one of us confides to the woman next to her (in the kind of whisper that is truly meant only for the person next to you but is so enticing that it draws in our whole group). This woman tells us that yes, she has done it—had anal sex—and that yes, it's really fun, it's fantastic even, and that it seems like a decent thing to explore if you're planning to have sex with the same person in pretty much the same ways for the rest of your life.

Before we know it we're onto the kinkier stuff that Becca promised when she and I spoke on the phone and I informed her that we are a group of mothers in their late-thirties and forties (the segue from middle-age suburban mothers to "kinkier stuff" making me smile there in the nursery school hallway where I fielded her call). The goods, though, aren't as kinky as I've imagined. First comes a very utilitarian-looking riding crop that seems silly and oddly highbrow, but that manages to entice Ruby and me into ordering one each.

The afternoon our packages arrive, I will grab the phone when the caller ID reports Ruby on the line. Here's what will have gone down in their house moments before:

(NINE-YEAR-OLD) DYLAN LIVINGSTON: Mom! Mom. You got a package. It's out on the porch.

RUBY: I saw that.
DYLAN: I'm pretty sure it's a lightsaber.
RUBY: It's not a lightsaber.
DYLAN: Looks like a lightsaber. It's a *looong* package. Could be a lightsaber.
RUBY: It's not a lightsaber.
DYLAN: What is it then?
RUBY: It's an umbrella.

The riding crop makes its way around the circle just before the Black Flogger, which is a sort of moplike flay with thin strips of black leather. My First Bondage Kit makes me laugh because it seems so like baby Lucas's *My First Word Book*, Hannah's My First Purse, and Xavier's My First Shaving Kit.

Becca then asks for a volunteer and I hope it's not for the clip thingies (for nipples? for scrotums?) that I spy in the kinky section of the catalog. Instead of clips, Becca unfurls a long black rope. In seconds willowy Simone is standing before us with her elbows bent overhead, hands tied behind her shoulder blades and then to her waist with the Good Vibrations Basic Bondage Rope. Becca cannot know, however, that Simone's height belies the almost freakish flexibility that had made her look so feline as she stalked on all fours across Catherine Rose's purple faux fur during erotic dance. With an effortless and eerily snakelike motion, Simone contorts herself free of Becca's expert knots. Our skilled facilitator can only articulate the very thing that we attendees have been thinking all evening: "I've never seen anything like that."

Perhaps wanting to finish with something more soothing than ropes and floggers and riding crops, Becca passes around an array of Massage Bars, lubes, creams, and edible "Body Dusts" that smell delicious. The little glass pot of Zing Pleasure Cream makes its way around the circle, each of us applying some to her lips because no one can resist its promise of "warming" and "tingling." Simone is the only one who doesn't immediately like the sensation. She sits with empty hands out to her sides. "Nothing!" She says. "I feel nothing!" which leads to teasing that her hyper-orgasmic self can't feel her lips tingling because all her nerve endings are concentrated in her clit. Even Simone, though—once the belated tingling begins—orders up some Zing. No sooner are we all warmed and tingling than Becca intimates that the cream is even better for nipple stimulation. The little pot then makes a second circuit, many of us pulling our shirts and bras forward to reach down the necks of T-shirts and up under the hems of sweaters to dab at our breasts, ooohing and aaahing and chuckling at the new sensation.

———

Alas, our collective pleasure will prove no guarantee of success in other venues. Some ten days after the party, I will receive the following e-mail (copied verbatim) from (Dr.) Katherine's husband, Paul:

"By the way, I was reading *Harper's* in bed the other night and Katherine whipped off my pants and put some cream on my popsicle. The cream was apparently manufactured by the same company that makes Ben-Gay. The burning sensation brought back memories of being tortured in the locker room of an all-boy Jesuit high school.

"I leapt from the bed and ran the 40-yard dash to the shower in four flat. Speaking of flat, my Johnson was very unhappy with the events and decided to turtle. Suffice it to say, the cream should be listed as a WMD: weapon of member destruction.

"The doctor may be sent to Guantanamo to torture Islamic terrorists.

"Hoping to sip wine and recover with you soon,

"Paul."

Minutes after reading Paul's e-mail and rushing out the door for after-school pickup, I will park behind Katherine, who will be signing off a cell phone call with "All right, okay, 'bye, Sweetie," before snapping her phone shut.

"Was that *Paul*?" I will cry in sympathy.

"That was Sarah," Katherine will say. "Paul and I are not exactly calling each other 'sweetie' right now." She will hoist her toddler onto her hip as I hustle Xavier along.

"You would not have believed it," she'll begin. "I don't tend to be the initiator. I'm usually not very aggressive. But I just got so excited about the box! I put the cream on him," here she leans close, "and on my vagina. Not a lot either. Just a little bit."

I articulate her mute, horror-struck expression. "Bad?"

"Bad! Maybe it's not meant for mucous membranes." (Though the Good Vibrations Zing Pleasure Cream is billed as "Tingly and non-irritating for clit or nipple stimulation; Long-lasting and pleasantly powerful; Slight citrus scent, natural ingredients." In the interest of full disclosure, I have had reports from two Pleasure Party–goers that the Zing went over smashingly with them.)

As Katherine and I rush toward the classrooms, she will look long at me before attempting to further qualify the fact that she and Paul weren't currently using pet names. "To be fair, he had had a couple of bad days at work. And our date night got canceled this week." Then Katherine will smile. "It wasn't any of that." She will giggle. "It was the cream. It was awful. It was just horrible."

The delicious smelling but tame bath fizzies and candles that make their way around the living room are an unwanted signal that we will soon return to normalcy, to a school night, to snoring or eager husbands. Nine-thirty has never rolled around so quickly. We make last-minute scrawls on full order forms and write checks in checkbooks unused to this kind of purchase. We good mommies prepare to collect ourselves, beginning to thank Becca with genuine, effusive gratitude at such impressive illumination on an ordinary Wednesday evening.

My own Open Enterprises package will arrive the same day as most everyone else's. Because Ruby and I together had experienced the same weird enthusiasm for the riding crop, both of us will receive the same "loooong" box. Unlike Dylan Livingston, however, my kids will remain blissfully uninterested.

The funny thing is, I will wait weeks to open the box. I will find that the plain brown carton itself (full of at least a dozen items whose specifics I've forgotten) will provide plenty of allure in its own right. There will be "box in a box on the counter" jokes. There will be mid–Private Time speculation about its contents and whispered allusion to some remembered toy or another.

There will be so much innuendo and anticipation that I will wonder one morning while handing the kids their waffles if Bill and I might be disappointed. But then I will remember the special soy candle with the lower burning point that allows you to drip wax on your partner without scorching the shit out of each other. This will sound silly there in my kitchen at seven-thirty in the morning. Sort of stupid really. But then . . . maybe not so silly. Maybe hot wax sounds sort of interesting. With the maple syrup poised over the first kid's plate I will think of the melting candle. I will consider the riding crop—which will actually get me going a little—and I will smile, pretty certain that the box will come through.

"Oh but you," Becca says as her preparing-to-leave hands go to her heart, "you guys are one of the best groups I've ever had."

"We are?" Simone's surprise is genuine.

"You probably think I say that to everyone, but really. You guys are seriously up there. With the equestrians . . . and the men-in-drag bachelorette party."

And I have the sense that Becca isn't bullshitting. I

imagine giggly bachelorettes—gay and straight. I'm curious about the equestrians, but chalk up their fabulousness to all that straddling (plus they probably have ordered a gross of riding crops). I envision young women who would have hired Becca after a class during which they finally "reclaimed" their orgasms from brutish frat guys. I consider groups of women who don't know their bodies with the thoroughness afforded by pregnancy and childbirth and the raising of children. I think of hip young adults who love sex but haven't experienced the intimacy, trust, and familiarity that are particular to monogamy. I want to have another party right away for the handful of mothers whose husbands had to work late this evening or whose babysitters flaked (parties are free, by the way; a facilitator like Becca works only on commission!). I want to sign up all of our men for an enlightening party of their own (to which Bill says, "No fucking way," when I finally make it upstairs and regale him with just a fraction of my newfound knowledge).

"We'll have you back again soon," I promise Becca, who stands joyful before us. "There are so many more of us who really really need you."

CHAPTER 16

Arguments Against

*[Parenting] requires taking on the new identity of parents and sub-
ordinating one's own needs to those of the infant. Amazingly, our
culture takes it as a given that this process will go smoothly, even
automatically. Nothing could be more misleading.*

—Judith S. Wallerstein and
Sandra Blakeslee
The Good Marriage

Okay, so poor Paul? With the burnt popsicle? He appears to have maintained enough manliness to put
his arguments against (which are mostly Paul's voicing of
Katherine's arguments against) into a quantified Top Reasons List reminiscent of John's. Here's Paul's response:

Top Reasons We Don't End Up Having Sex

7. "I feel fat. I did not exercise today. I just had dinner and then I ate
   some of the kids' leftover hot dogs. I just saw Katie Fergussen jog
   by. I feel fat."
6. "I want to read my book because the noise and activity level of
   the kids approximates a daily domestic hurricane."
5. "Your mother called. She gave me a lot of very 'helpful' advice."

4. *Grey's Anatomy*.
3. "I'm too worried about the kids' summer camp schedule and whether or not we should get our garage finished."
2. "You have been on a business trip and we haven't talked for more than five minutes in two weeks . . . and you want to have sex!"
1. Unstated: "When you drove the kids to school, I masturbated in the shower. My mojo is gone until my boys can refill the tank."

PART FOUR

The Backside

CHAPTER 17

Viva Las Vegas!

He suggests Las Vegas for his thirty-fifth birthday and she looks up from the baby bottle she's trying to jam the scrub brush into.

"Really?" she asks.

"Sure. It'll be great."

It's true that he has claimed, in hammered phone calls from the Hard Rock or The Palms during guys' weekends, that he wants to go to Las Vegas with her sometime.

Putting the scrub brush down, settling for an ineffectual rinsing of the bottle, she imagines the dim and frenzied interior of a casino-cum-bar-cum-strip-club. Cigarette smoke hangs in toxic layers over dancers who intimidate her with their leggy, fake-rack bodies. The idea of it makes her feel like a big loser. No one reads in Las Vegas. Everyone stays up really late. She would far rather sleep than gamble, which she's never done before. Gambling involves math and strategy, and she's horrible at math and strategy.

She pulls her shoulders back and takes a deep breath. To-gether they plan Las Vegas because she loves him and it's his thirty-fifth birthday and hearing him say, sober and heartfelt in the kitchen, that he wants to go to Las Vegas alone with her is enough to make her say she'll go.

She tells friends they're going to Las Vegas. A couple of them groan. Most tell her she's sooo lucky and she'll have an amazing time. She relates more to the groaners because the coordination of babysitters and playdates even for a sin-gle kids' overnight at her parents' is overwhelming. She's packing weekend bags less for herself (what does one wear in Las Vegas?) than for the three kids whose needs vary from specific Game Boy cartridges to specific nightgowns to specific baby bottles, even though the youngest is two and a half and shouldn't probably be having two to three (to five) bottles of milk daily. She's hassled because her precious morning reading time has been cut into by copying out schedules with dozens of phone numbers. Then when it comes time to write that letter To Whom it May Concern giving her mother permission to seek medical care for her children, she envisions catastrophic broken bones and fevers of 104 degrees that indicate horrid unnameable dis-eases.

She tells people she's never been to Las Vegas before. Which isn't entirely true. They had gone when they were first dating. But it was a trip with her parents, which made it not count. Her dad had business and the four of them had flown down together. They ate in nice restaurants and they saw some Cirque du Soleil or another, but it never felt like Vegas. The only time it came close to feeling like the fabled (and daunting) desert oasis was when her parents stopped by her and Bill's sumptuous room at Caesar's on the way to dinner. Her father strolled in with her mother; Bill was in the bathroom. Her father stepped up onto the silly platform under the vast bed, sat down on the high mattress, crossed his arms behind his head, and fell backwards.

"Whoooa!" cried Freeman as Bill emerged from the loo. "They gave you two the serious setup." Her father pointed up at the center of the heavily draped canopy to the mirrored ceiling they had assumed was standard in every bedroom but had not, in fact, come with her parents' accommodations.

And who's to say if the trip to Las Vegas for his birthday coincided with one of those periods—sometimes lasting a week, sometimes months—when they couldn't keep their hands off each other, or if the trip to Las Vegas actually generated one of those phases. Not giving the question its due until afterward when things got ugly, she found herself elated even before the plane left the ground in drizzly San Jose. The fifty-minute flight was filled not with children but with furtive making out and twenty-five minutes of uninterrupted Edith Wharton. Las Vegas was seventy-eight degrees and sunny in late January and the stark Nevada desert reminded her of her Nona and Granddad whom she adored and who lived in Reno, where she spent a lot of time as a girl.

And as it turns out, the general population in the Las Vegas airport was not intimidating or avant in any remotely threatening way. The carpet underfoot felt new and plush and the huge screens advertising shows and hotels and restaurants produced in her an actual thrill.

The taxi ride to the Four Seasons took eight minutes. The lobby was decorated with luxuriant palms and hushed tones, high ceilings and fanciful arrangements of Dr. Seuss–like flowers that captivated her. In their room on the thirty-eighth floor she found something deeply alluring in the filtered greenish light, in the way the windows stretched all the way to the floor. They had good sex after which he needed to take a quick call. She felt—remarkably—no urge to pick up her book. She stood by the windows with a glass of red wine and watched evening creep over the desert. Content, she sang softly to herself, "Viva Las Vegas," the Dead Kennedys singing backup in her head. Quietly she sang, "Viva, Viva Las Vegas," realizing then that she actually wanted him to hurry up and finish his call. She had loved the energy of the casino they had traversed, the thick carpets underfoot, the massive crystal chandeliers that she found strangely beautiful. It was as she gazed over the spreading dun desert that the immense rectangular pool below her erupted and became a skillfully orchestrated, masterfully managed show of spouting arcs of colorfully lit water that actually made her, there at the window, well up with tears.

The glass of wine was followed by a few cocktails at the blackjack tables where an unpredictable eleven of their twenty-three Las Vegas hours would be spent. She surprised them both by being the one who wanted to skip *Zumanity* because of how clever and truly entertaining her husband was in his table talk, because of how much they felt like a team when he signaled what she ought to do with each vexing sixteen, because they finished their blackjack marathon five hundred dollars up. Their dinner at Smith and Wollensky was maybe the best meal she had eaten in her life: a football-sized "cracklin' pork shank" that arrived on a white platter without any garnish at all save a six-inch bowie knife sticking out the top. More blackjack led to practically fucking in the elevator because of the energy they had accumulated all evening, which led to watching some excellent porn and a good (if seriously truncated) night's sleep on a mattress that she still talks about to this day.

The next morning they flew home.

Where each quarreling child's voice—the kids were two and four and six during this first trip to Las Vegas—seemed brutally amplified. The mere specter of packing her kindergartener's lunch for Monday morning brought her almost to tears. She chalked it up to hangover, though she actually felt fine. She was sullen and removed and yelled at them on Sunday night when they balked at a preposterous six-thirty bedtime, then felt awful because they had seemed so happy to have her back when she wasn't the tiniest bit happy to be back.

"I'm losing my mind," she whispered to him on the phone on Monday after ferrying her children to and from school and soccer and ice skating and Music Together. "I swear to God I am not up to this."

"You are. It's hard."

"I need to go away with you." There on the living-room couch she closes her eyes. "We need to go away. This weekend."

"I'm not sure that's realistic."

She thinks she might cry. She sniffs so he knows she thinks she might cry.

"Maybe the answer," he says, "is to get more of that kind of thing in our lives here."

She stares out over the Polly Pockets and Legos and blocks

littering the floor. And this is not even the playroom. This is the living room, the only designated adult space in the whole house. She took refuge in this adult space earlier, trying in vain to nurture memories of a certain soaring and lush palm-and-sandstone lobby. But the living room was infiltrated when the three of them had trailed in, hungry for her.

"Maybe you're right." She sniffs again, disappointed that her bleakness is failing to generate even a single cathartic tear. "I guess you're right."

She doesn't feel appreciably better until after she meets her friend Meg for coffee on Wednesday, their toddlers in tow at a local café where the kids can run around a fountain that she keeps gazing at, blocking the children out with a flat upraised hand in an effort to recapture the strange poignancy of the water show she had loved on the desert.

"I really do think Bill's right," says Meg. "You know, when Renzo and I got back from Italy last summer I was in such a funk. I thought of this song that I loved there. It's this Italian song, kind of goofy, about creating Venice in your own backyard. That sounds so goofy. Maybe it wasn't exactly that. But that's the idea." Meg grabbed her toddler's arm and shoved another bite of croissant into his drooly mouth. "We've been trying to do that. Even if it's just coffee after dinner. I clear the table and get out the nice cups and saucers and it feels like we're still in Florence."

But cups and saucers don't evoke seas of perfect green baize or pumped-in oxygen or prescient blackjack dealers from Tonopah who help you win. Las Vegas was an alternate universe where there was no need to pay attention to anyone's bedtime, least of all her own. She had not, once, not in twenty-three unprecedented hours, felt her usually constant urge to read.

This week she has risen each morning at four-thirty to desperately indulge in *Infinite Jest* before forcing herself from the solace of intellect to wake the children at seven. She has been testy and quick with the kids. She has been testy and quick with her husband. Because here in suburbia she can't make out with him in the only elevator they ever ride. It's the elevator to the bookstore café they visit every Saturday morning and it rises a single floor. This might even be enough time in that other universe to wrangle a kiss or cop his package, but the elevator ride in her tree-lined town is not only brief but also full of her two-, four- and six-year-old, first fighting over who gets to push the buttons then alternately yelling and shushing as they try to time their little kid jumps (her husband also dismayingly absorbed in this) to coincide with the elevator's gravity-enhancing halt.

She can't, she realizes, even have coffee with her husband after dinner the way Meg does with Renzo. Bill doesn't like coffee. Or tea. Hot drinks make him hot. Post-dinner is a time her husband enthusiastically devotes to coloring books and blocks and wrestling. She thinks they ought to get a date night going again but their only babysitter moved back to Brazil, their babysitter being their only babysitter because this mom has historically been very much the martyr, insisting that she didn't have children only to have a babysitter raise them. The way she tries to shoulder all her children's care, though, isn't doing anyone any good.

What works is a different comment of Meg's. "This is my new thing," she says when their café conversation comes around to HEM and *Exile in Guyville* and what other music these two friends love lately. "Renzo got me an iPod for

Christmas. I listen to it constantly. I swear it's like adding a really great soundtrack to your crazy life. I just pretend the kids are the conflict part of some goofy romantic comedy or something. It's the best."

Last time they had met for coffee Meg had revealed that she and her husband were trying to have sex every day. "It's like going for a jog," Meg had explained. "It never sounds like that good an idea beforehand, but then you're into it and you think, 'This isn't bad.' Then you really get going and it's not bad at all. When you're done? You feel great all day!" (Ed Duane had once recommended a different tack: "It's straight up supply and demand," he declared while poking at a tri-tip on the grill. "You just don't give it to 'em all that often," which really got to his wife, Nikki—though this approach of course may backfire with husbands who are more interested in sex than their wives. "Keep the supply low," Ed's theory went, "and the demand stays high.")

So although she doesn't own an iPod, there is a moment— linked to Las Vegas—when music reenters her life. Her husband has always been the musical one, splitting time between espn.com and the iTunes store once the latter revolutionized music acquisition. Precious chunks of his time are spent trolling for new bands. He rises from the computer in the office with some new track at high volume only to turn on a CD in the living room then the stereo in the bedroom, different songs blaring through each space. As much as she wants to embrace the music (and him), the conflicting drum beats and guitar riffs and lyrical strains conspire with the kids' voices to drive her crazy. So she follows him, children trailing and needing her and sometimes charming her with their impromptu dancing as she moves through rooms turning off stereos to create less noise but being sure to leave—echoes of Las Vegas—one source of music intact.

She tells him Meg's daily sex suggestion and they smile, figuring that what with his travel they pretty much have sex every day he's around anyway. The soundtrack-for-your-life-idea, though, is the one she underscores and she is touched when he spends much thought compiling her a CD that she listens to devotedly (mostly loud in the car where it drowns out the kids who sometimes sing along, which makes her feel good even when the lyrics may be of questionable taste). She loves the idea that he has chosen these songs for her and that he has ripped and burned the same CD for himself, this CD connecting them even as he is driving to the office, she to ice skating and soccer and baseball, dentists and doctors and playdates. These CDs are significant in their musical content because the songs he chooses make her feel more like his wife than the mother of his children, the collection like an update of the mix tapes best friends made for each other in middle school.

She falls in love with Beck and The Decemberists, Damien Rice and Wolfmother, Sufjan Stevens and Cat Power and Joshua James. She finds herself actually looking forward to piling the kids into the car because it is there, her attention focused and the music close, where she is most easily transformed. It is there she can evoke the kind of renewal and regeneration and let's-fuck-in-the-shower-or-the-elevator energy she had felt in Las Vegas. Even in a song's opening bars—Iron & Wine's plaintive acoustic guitar or old school AC/DC's heavy percussion—the music transforms her. This is transformation that she can control, that she chooses, that is ever at her fingertips. It is magical.

She recalls a moment in graduate school when her beloved Professor Dougherty stated that yes, this passage in Galdós elicited pathos but that music actually evoked emotion most effectively. She took offense. Literature was surely the best way to convey feeling! Yet hadn't she spent that whole fall semester (having miscarried in late August) listening to *The Wall* over and over for how it made her hopelessness feel soothed and amplified and understood?

Music in the car leads to music on the patio where they have a new settee and a pair of chairs with inviting cream-colored cushions that make her want to sit outdoors on summer evenings while the dishes are left to crust up until morning. They hang out that summer with people who love music even more than they do. These people speak intelligently and interestingly about bands. These people do that thing where the silence between tracks gives way to a song and someone's face shows blissful recognition and the person says, "This song is *so* good."

They start calling the patio the loggia. They start calling these friends—most of whom are musicians, some in gig-playing bands—"Music Club."

Here's how it works: Each Music Club meeting has a theme, say "Outstanding Cover," or "Seminal Heavy Metal," "Indecipherable Lyrics," a "Jimi Hendrix Intensive," or "A-Song-That's-So-Good-You-Actually-Look-Forward-to-Your-Commute-or-the-Third-Carpool-of-the-Day-Because-You-Can-Listen-to-It-Loud-in-the-Car." The couple that hosts is given the task of compiling members' choices on a single CD, a copy of which is given to each couple . . . a party favor of sorts.

Music Club itself becomes transformative. Almost literally. During the Hendrix Intensive Kate suggests that the only way to really experience *Are you Experienced?* is to lie on the floor in the dark. Off go the lights. They all lie together on the resounding hardwood, eyes closed, each having reverted to late adolescence . . . until the kids come in and pile on. The Masturbation Songs meeting creates metamorphosis of specific songs themselves: Closer analysis of Jackson Browne's "Rosie" reveals that he's referring to his own palm and Lucinda Williams's "Right in Time" sounds forever different after one member's careful explication of lyrics. Passionate lip-syncing at Seminal Heavy Metal makes for rockstar transformation and every meeting sees each member momentarily transformed into serious music critic. When her husband suggests "Dance" as a theme, it's the perfect opportunity to wear not only the ultra-short faux-Pucci dress that fellow-music-clubber Ruby had given her, but also the black wig she was sure made her look exactly like Uma Thurman in *Pulp Fiction*, except maybe just slightly less striking and a couple of feet shorter.

As any Music Club member might have predicted, Dance gets particularly raucous. Sure, there's less conversation and thus fewer points of meaningful lyric interpretation. Sure, Kate's slaved-over salmon and elegant table go underappreciated. But babysitters have been hired and makeup applied and work is left early so that the moment when "Starry Eyed Surprise" is piped at full volume into the dining room and four of the six attending Music Club members involuntarily rise from their seats to dance, all members would agree that there has occurred a valuable no-longer-just-a-mother/father/doctor/banker/engineer transformation.

Transformation continues when chairs are pushed back and napkins thrown down. Kate leads the other girl members up the stairs and into her bathroom, which foray itself creates intimacy because how many adults venture en masse into the master bath of friends they have known for under a year? While one member takes a desperately needed pee (because Dance has involved plentiful libations), there are comments from the toilet about that amazing phenomenon wherein a mom can go for hours needing to pee but cannot find a single second—in her own home!—to leave the kids and take care of it. This observation leads to the universal awe and irritation women harbor at men's need to spend half an hour on the can while all kinds of kid-related hell breaks loose around them. The one member is pulling up underwear and the other is trying on Kate's lipstick, pouting at herself in the master bath mirror when their hostess sallies out of the closet with an armload of wigs.

Further transformation. Hip-length platinum waves for Kate, a distinctly Jackie O. fall that is amazing with Katherine's dark locks, the black Uma Thurman number cast aside for a sleek white-blond look.

And, though she fails to recall the details of the conversation—Dance having been perhaps the most inebriated she's been since college—she apparently made mention, as the women peered into the bathroom mirror at the same shade of lipstick on three mouths, that she had never kissed a girl.

There had, of course, been dreams. Once when she was pregnant and was awakened by an excellent involuntary orgasm. She had dreamt of an all-girls' high school classmate. The two of them had pressed their hips and tummies and chests together but did not kiss because somehow both understood that kissing would have ruined how good it all felt. Not that there hadn't been kissing dreams. But just one or two. The kind of dream that had seemed vaguely shameful the next morning.

The dreams had come, she was sure, from energy generated by those girls that she had harbored a kind of crush on. Like sensual Georgie from Marin (who committed suicide at twenty by jumping off the Golden Gate Bridge). These girl crushes were not like the real crushes on the real boys she really wanted to kiss. The girl crushes were abstract and subtle, like her crush on Beck or Maggie Gyllenhaal. The type of crush that made her happy when whichever woman (lamentably never Beck or Maggie) called on the phone or appeared in her children's elementary school hallways. Not crushes that meant she was physically attracted to these women. Less physical desire than a slightly charged joy. Because the thought of making out with another woman was mostly repellent. The thought of a vag anywhere near her mouth? Yuck.

But so Kate and Andrew's living room is thumping on that night of Dance. Lit with pulsing colored disco lights and fog from the fog machine that is especially impressive in combination with Andrew's DJ-grade strobe light, the suburban space becomes their own big-city club. Music having been equaled this evening by the importance of bodies. Dance transforms both men and women. (This is most certainly a group of parents. Only a father of relatively young kids would have once said, as Andre had, "Mucous Plug" in lieu of Music Club, the group jovially attending "Mucous Plug" gatherings for the next half year.) Yet these middle-age mothers are graduates of in-home erotic dance classes. They may be flabby and five pounds too heavy, they may have crow's feet and laugh lines, but they have given each other lap dances. They are well aware of the power of women's bodies together. Both alone and with an audience of men. All six of these parental bodies are moving in ways that these bodies almost never move anymore.

They are dancing to Akon. She and Kate. Their faces are close. Then further away. They are dancing with hands held and hips close. They are vaguely aware of being watched. This music is not slow, the music is a percussive, heavy remix of "Smack That," and the refrain makes them pull apart, hips dipping. They draw close again. Then closer. A hand finds a shoulder and she and Kate are kissing. They move away with laughter and unnecessary apology and then they kiss again.

It isn't until later that night, arriving home with her husband, that having kissed Kate seems like anything out of the ordinary. She and her husband are undressed before they're up the stairs because the kids are at her parents' and the two of them are practically fucking on the stairs because of all the dancing and the music and the drinking. Their ears are ringing like they've just been to a major concert and they are sweaty and when she says, as though surprised, "I kissed Kate," he pulls her down the hallway toward the bedroom saying, "Yeah. I saw."

But it's in Las Vegas—suddenly her favorite city, the two of them visiting three times that calendar year, once with her parents and siblings and siblings-in-law (kids left behind) for the late August vacation she unpredictably suggested, rebutting their objections to 110 degree weather with "It's not like we'll ever be outside"—but of course it's during yet another trip to Vegas that she meets Dana. Dana is a friend of the friends who planned the trip.

Dana suddenly seems to be making kind of a big deal out of the fact that she has "never kissed a girl." She and

Dana have been talking, coincidentally, about music. The two of them sit close. There are three couples, six of them total, just like "Dance." But this is a real club, this is the renowned Spearmint Rhino, the upscale Las Vegas strip joint you actually have to get into a cab and onto a freeway to visit.

The two of them sit talking, dressed disconcertingly alike in tight expensive jeans, strappy high heels and skimpy tops, both blond and somehow obviously from California. The club is playing some kind of looping remake of "Sexual Healing," which nonsensically leads to talk of Alexi Murdoch, then no more rationally to R.E.M., which leads to reminiscence of the punk and New Wave and Ska they had loved when coming of age at rivalrous northern and southern points in the Golden State.

She doesn't know how the conversation wends to Dana saying she's never kissed a girl. Immediately there arises Kate's post-Dance axiom that once a girl tells you she's never kissed another girl, that pretty much means she wants to kiss a girl. There in the club she might have even recited some aspect of this phenomenon to her newfound Bobbsey Twin. It may be the way they have to lean close to talk over loud music that is almost always but not quite her favorite Dance track. It may be that nearly naked women are dancing and swinging around them on platforms and small stages, when not pressing large breasts and shapely hips into men seated in the bucket-type chairs that surround them.

So she leans over and Dana sees what's coming. Dana smiles and leans closer and the two of them kiss.

There is an odd moment afterward. Dana says that the kiss was . . . kind of . . . forceful. Dana has always thought that kissing a girl was supposed to be . . . more soft and . . . gentle. While our initiator is at first taken aback, maybe even a little hurt, she then realizes that Dana's kissing was entirely too soft, too delicate for her tastes. She is thinking to herself that her husband is a way better kisser than Dana. It was nice, sure, because it was different, but kissing Dana was too subtle and tentative. She wondered, did Dana kiss her husband like that?

But so she looks over to see just what kind of magic this kiss has worked on her husband, who has indeed seen his wife kissing Dana. But there's maybe too much other stuff going on in the room. She has just kissed her new friend and though it was mostly for herself and Dana, it was also for their men. Across the small round table, though, her husband appears more interested in the professionals around them. When she moves closer and asks if he saw, he smiles and kisses her. He pulls her close to sit on his chair between his legs. He kisses her again and tells her that it was sort of hot, sure, but that it just seemed a little silly.

Which, were they not in her favorite alternate universe and in another of the phases when they can't keep their hands off each other, might have caused self-conscious dismay.

What apparently seems less silly to him, what probably distracted her husband from realizing how totally sexy his wife was while kissing their new friend Dana, is the idea of his wife in close proximity to one of the nearly naked, extremely well-endowed professionals in their midst.

He pulls her yet closer and asks who she likes the best.

Charcy.

Charcy is the name the stripper gives when she asks. It's such an odd name, so ungainly for this pretty woman that

she assumes it's the stripper's real name despite her cer-
tainty that each of these women has some kind of porn-star
alias that's crucial for the detachment their profession demands.

She also chooses to believe Charcy's southern lilt because
she's a sucker for accents and linguistic variance of any ilk.
She chooses to believe the accent but not the white blond
hair. She believes that Charcy has come from New Orleans
after Katrina, but she doesn't believe the artifice of the
breasts. Distracted by the oddity of the name, she finally
satisfies herself by imagining parents, named Chuck and
Darcy, each wanting to stake a claim on their uncommonly
pretty baby girl.

While her husband visits one of the many many cash
machines situated throughout this rather small establishment, she and the stripper sit talking. They are both blond,
but nowhere near Bobbsey Twins, what with Charcy's long-
sleeved but midriff-bearing, thin white cotton turtleneck
that snugs round breasts and appears far more straight-up
sexy than the plum-colored Elie Tahari silk camisole she
packed back in California for how it felt both sophisticated
and revealing.

In her husband's absence, They are less lap dancer and
lap dancee than the soul-baring kind of friend one makes
on airplanes and in pediatric waiting rooms. The discovery
that they each have three kids and a husband they thinks is
hot and good makes for such bonding that she feels like she
could tell Charcy the most guarded secrets (though she can
think of none).

Even as her husband returns and Charcy moves closer to
her, the conversation continues. Charcy's hands are on the
back of the chair, her bare knee pressing between blue-jeaned

ones. And unlike the loutish, puffy, mustached men whose hands lie inert and creepy on the arms of their chairs, her hands are lifted by Charcy. Her palms are pressed to Charcy's ribcage and though she understands that this pretty, kind woman is only doing her job, she's sure that Charcy's hand pressing into the back of her neck means Charcy is actually enjoying herself.

And Charcy's skin is so smooth! Charcy comes forward and presses closer, hands invited to travel around, down the narrowing of Charcy's waist and onto the curve of her hips. Charcy's round cotton-clad breasts press, then, against her flat chest.

And Charcy smells good. Like some high-end moisturizer that's really pleasant despite the thought that it's surely stipulated in these women's contracts that they smell good. And have fresh breath. Which leads to thoughts of how really nasty some men in this club must smell, and creates yet more solidarity. Meanwhile, Charcy is speaking softly into her ear saying that sure it's hard to spend evenings away from the kids but that the littlest one has a cold right now so it's not all bad to be out of the house.

And Charcy tells her that this is fun, that she likes this. Which doesn't sound like a lie. Even though it's her job and she's probably full of crap, Charcy smells good and seems so friendly and she thinks she'd like to sit talking with Charcy and feeling Charcy's skin and hips and her breasts pressed up against her for longer than the single song her husband has purchased for twenty bucks.

Charcy sits back a little then. With legs spread she cocks her head and says, "You are so pretty. I swear. You could get a job here, you know." Which is ridiculous. But flattering too. Charcy is saying that it's great she comes here with her husband. That it's really good for them to be doing this stuff together. The remix sounds like "I See Right Through to You" and is loud enough that she feels the music in her chest. She loves this song and Charcy is coming forward, closer, saying that she likes dancing with her more than men because she likes talking to girls—most girls but not all girls—because she feels comfortable with girls.

She tells herself that Charcy is fishing for another song (far from the bad-breath louts) and a big tip. But Charcy's lilt is compelling and Charcy's hands are guiding hers upward to her ribs again. Charcy's cheek against hers turns out to be just as soft as the skin on Charcy's tummy and this all feels unbelievably good. This is license to arch up a little, which makes Charcy moan and Charcy says she's getting hot—and this is of course more bullshit, but it doesn't matter because this is like listening to really good music or watching porn.

This is her body overriding her mind. And her hands are on Charcy's breasts. Charcy leans close and her big tits are full, the skin soft. No part of her husband's body or her flat-chested body feels like Charcy's breasts. She almost wishes that her husband could feel these unbelievable tits because that would really make his night, but she's the only one who gets to touch Charcy's body and apparently it's legal to touch the strippers after all. The round breasts in her hands feel really unbelievably good, and she is getting more and more aroused and this is transformative. This is new terrain even in this parallel desert universe and they will leave Nevada the next morning but she will bring this with her.

Into their minimalist bedroom with kids banished to the other side of the Private Time door. Into the proscribed and mundane world that makes her feel safe and competent and valued. She will remember how good Charcy smelled and how she honestly thought they could have been friends. In the suburban bedroom she remembers the fullness of those breasts against her palms, the skin like suede but warm and firm and there in bed she'll whisper to him, "I pressed my hands so hard against those tits."

She will say to her husband, "I rolled my hands outward," and "I want to press my palms into her breast just one more time." He will have his own visual of his wife cupping those big fucking tits. This is suburbia but she will whisper that she wants to suck on those tits. She'll say aloud that she wants to push them together and run her tongue between them. She will be getting closer and closer to coming without so much as a vibrator in hand. She knows how good Charcy smelled and her husband never will and this is transformative. It's also like some kind of orgasm trigger. She talks about wanting to press those tits together while he fucks them with his hard cock and she comes and he comes.

Afterward, she will lie there in their ordinary bed in her ordinary house.

Content, she will sing very softly, sleepily, mostly to herself, "Viva Las Vegas . . ." The large breasts and good-smelling skin will be replaced with drowsy thoughts of the detergent and eggs she needs to buy that afternoon at the market. She will continue, though, softly singing to herself, "Viva, viva Las Vegas."

CHAPTER 18

Arguments Against

It is all too easy to let the marital relationship erode when children take center stage.

—Judith S. Wallerstein and
Sandra Blakeslee
The Good Marriage

I don't suppose you've forgotten beautiful Kate? The one who got lost on her way to Hacienda Cuatro? The one I kissed at Dance. So we were on the back patio talking and watching our girls play "House" when I asked her for any arguments against. Kate, being thoughtful, considered the question. Just then the kids had a total fit about who got to be the mom (which seemed ironic). The pizza guy arrived at the back gate and the dog got out and I couldn't find my wallet and so the question, naturally, got lost.

In the early darkness of the next morning I received the following e-mail:

You asked for arguments against sex? Here are some thoughts.

Feeling disconnected from one another by life . . .
bills, kids, laundry, packing lunches, walking dogs. I
think, for a lot of people (or at least the anal retentive variety such as myself), these things have a way of skewing
your priorities so that the day-to-day to-do list can seem
more immediately important than investing in your relationship.

Letting go. I know that I, at least, have trouble putting
things aside. Things like the fact that he went to bed
early when I stayed up to get everything ready for the
kids in the morning. Or that he drank too much and left
me to clean up after a dinner party. Or that he didn't get
out of bed when we had kids over for a slumber party
who were up and hungry at 7:00. I know it's wrong to do
this, but when these things build up over time it can be
hard to let them go and "surrender" to sex.

Losing track of your own sexuality. Frankly, between
playing the roles of mother, wife, daughter, daughter-in-
law, employee, school volunteer, driver, nurse, chaperone,
cleaning lady, etc., I sometimes feel like I'm a completely
different person from the one who used to feel desirable,
alluring, spontaneous, and sexually confident before the
kids came.

Going too long. Not just between the times when you
actually "do it," but between the times you feel really intimate with one another. Once you lose your rhythm, it's
hard to get it back. As a result, sex and intimacy can feel
awkward, forced, planned ("every date night"), or obliga-
tory rather than fun, spontaneous, and perfectly natural
(as it used to).

How's all that . . . for arguments against?

CHAPTER 19

Jealousy

A few days after a Music Club overnight at Ruby's Sonoma County get away, my mom and I are having one of the many cups of tea we have together during the course of any given week. We stand in my kitchen, evening having fallen, the heater's first rumblings making me realize that the room has grown a little cold.

"There's something"—my mother slows her movements, leans against a counter—"I want to mention. I've been thinking about this lately. I wanted to mention it."

Because she is oracular and uncommonly wise, I also still. I prepare for what will be some kind of gem but that sounds more ominous than the encouraging and supportive tack my mother invariably takes with me. I imagine devastating news: the discovery of a lump in her breast or her keen psychologist's eye having observed something worrisome in one of my kids. "What?" I ask.

"Just that there are studies, and I have noticed with my clients, that couples in their late thirties and early forties are particularly vulnerable to marital infidelity."

Now, this is the thoughtful woman who reassured me when I was suffering through my first never-sleeping infant that Bill's long hours did not mean he was having an affair. "He's not," she had promised then, "one you need to worry about." Eight years after such a comforting proclamation, this latest news is unsettling. Sure, the report from the Music Club overnight sounded a little wild: group-choreographed dance numbers, midnight skinny dipping in the lake, very little sleep, and a lot of drinking, the last of which must have been evident when Bill and I showed up at my parents' to collect the kids the morning after.

"Oh," I say. I am relieved at no cancer proclamation but surprised and a little put off that she might see anything suspect in my actions. Besides, Bill and I have never been more enamored of each other. "That's interesting," I continue, accepting her view as inviolable, which is what I do with my mother. I want, though, to set parameters on a trend that doesn't seem to apply to me. "I guess that makes sense for the general population. People having more energy when young kids become less of a focus. Couples maybe having drifted apart, or gotten bored with each other."

"Mmm-hmm."

"But you and I have talked about how Bill and I have never been happier. We've been having so much fun lately."

She nods, smiles sagely.

Wanting to close such a disconcerting conversation I say, "Something to keep in mind, I guess."

Later that night I give Bill an exaggerated, incredulous version, wanting him to tell me that my wise mother is being absurd, which he—with a little guidance—pretty much does. The next day I sink a little further into how her admonition felt unnecessary. I call Ruby and Kate just to have a few Music Clubbers in on what seems alarmist. I'm happy to have their agreement that we're not a bunch of spouse-swapping swingers. We're just good friends having a good time.

Not until later does the real worry creep in.

Unless, of course, you count the dream. Always the same dream. The dream of not being able to find him.

In real life, in June 1991, the Hanover Plain had cleared of all but seniors, which felt surreal. Only a thousand kids on campus was both exhilarating and disquieting. The knowledge that we would soon be thrust from our snug little college into an unknown and often hostile-seeming world became more real by the day. R.E.M.'s "The End of the World as We Know It" had just been released, which seemed prophetic. We all knew all the words. We sang them together in basements and bedrooms and the skanky kitchens of condemned communal houses.

During that semi-ecstatic evening hour before my roommates and I headed out for one of Senior Week's many festivities, I lounged preparty on Liz's bed looking through a stack of photos from her boyfriend's fraternity basement a few evenings before. There in the stack of at least a hundred totally juvenile shots was a picture of a man who was so handsome it gave me pause.

"Who," I asked Liz, "is this?"

She looked over my shoulder. "That's Bill."

"I just might," I said as I separated the photo from the stack, "have to meet this Bill."

My eventual unease came not until six months later when Bill and I had professed our love, had finally slept together, and had made allusions to the type of dog we might own together someday. The unease came from how easily I might never have seen that photograph. I could have decided not to join my girlfriends on that fateful night's "circuit" (a stop in each of a dozen basements, a beer chugged in every one, the majority of which beverages I slyly dumped onto the already-flooded cement floor). What if my friend Heidi had peeled off at the eighth fraternity instead of taking me down into Bill's basement to introduce us? What if Bill had been making out with someone when Heidi and I descended into the crowded space where he and I were mutually stunned.

Bill gave up on the ninety-one beers he was supposed to drink that week of June 1991. We had a picnic in the graveyard the next afternoon, during which his totally regal English professor strode by on a distant path, calling out to us (a Brontë citation that my Bill actually recognized from a course he had taken): "Play with the scented flower, / The young tree's supple bough / And leave my human feelings / In their own course to flow." Blaming flakiness on the magnitude of my sudden crush, I skipped out on that evening's girls' night for a party at Bill's house and a (relatively chaste) night in his bed. Two days later he headed to New

York for investment banking and I to California to teach high school, but something vital had begun.

In the dream I roam Hanover. I rush across gravel paths that intersect the college green. I enter hushed libraries. I climb centuries-old dormitory staircases to ask strangers or my closest friends where he is. They don't understand, though, because I am only capable of an inaudible whispering. Or they can make no sense of the words that are clear to me but sound like gibberish to anyone else. I wake without finding him.

Worse nightmares date from the dark tiny-baby era. I dream of my fatigued husband delivering the ominous "There's something I have to tell you." (Never "There's someone else," which—like the urban myth of never dreaming your death because you'll actually die—seems far too grave.) More disturbing are graphic dreams of walking into the small and shadowy dining room (always the dining room, for no good reason) in the little house in Oakland to realize that the writhing mass of something inhuman is my husband fucking another woman.

I wake from these dreams and pull myself to his sleep-warm body. "I had the dream," I tell him.

"I'm sorry," he says. I hear the smile in his voice that means the dream is totally unimportant. The dream, he communicates when he pulls me to him, has no bearing whatsoever on the loyalty with which he loves me.

We usually end up fucking and I usually end up feeling better. I laugh sort of sadly afterward at how stupid the dream is, the important thing being that it was just that: a dream.

Then comes this caveat from my omnipotent and omniscient mother. A scientific, clinically proven phenomenon rears its horrible head. I find myself obsessing about her warning while driving carpools. Rumors of phantom affairs are whispered by friends and acquaintances all around me. A close-knit neighborhood just south of ours is shaken when the husband of one couple and the wife of another (the couples having been the best of friends) have an affair that means the end of one marriage and serious damage to the other. Kate's friend Danielle (Sex Ed Danielle from Southern California) leaves her husband of seventeen years because sex is a priority for her and they're having no sex and she's therefore finished with monogamy.

I console myself with the idea that these marriages— outspokenly so in Danielle's case—were unhappy long before they ended in infidelity. I had recently spent a long evening at Kate's house with Danielle and Kate's friend Marla, who were talking about their experiences of infidelity. As Danielle and Marla spoke, they were animated, fervent, cathartic. But with some relief I realized that their situations were markedly different from mine: Each had registered serious misgivings as early as her wedding night. Each had ignored marital dissatisfactions while devoting herself entirely to babies. Each had emerged from the challenge of parenting very young children to understand that she did not love her husband, that realization sparked in both women's cases by infidelity that she initiated. Each spoke of liberation—of having freed herself from a passionless marriage—that felt hard-won and empowering. But their experiences sounded brutal to me . . . painful and complicated and scary. There in Kate's living room I reminded myself that I had never been more elated or content or optimistic than on my wedding night. I reminded myself that I have thought—on more occasions than I care to admit—that I'd surely toss the kids out of the proverbial life raft, wanting to keep only Bill to myself. I sat listening with respect and sympathy, but also rationalizing—despite what seemed ubiquitous rumors—that no one I knew personally was having an affair. Maybe the talk of infidelity wasn't concrete evidence of pervasive adultery so much as a concern for marriage that people seemed to suddenly share (or maybe not so suddenly, maybe suddenly only for me).

At parties and dinners and Music Club meetings I found myself nearly as energized and content and passionate as before. But I had begun to pay a new kind of attention.

Like the attention that leads to sickening deflating jealousy when a roomful of holiday cocktail-goers in my own December living room is silenced—drinking, grinning, listing—when Kate rises in her long blond wig before us.

The game is "Would You Rather." The question: Seal your head in a bag of vomit for fifteen minutes or bathe in a tub full of crap. Paralyzed by fear of stomach sickness, I—along with the majority of my guests—am arguing in favor of the quick dip in shit.

But there before us stands newly blond but always pretty Kate, suddenly affecting an accent that may or may not be southern but that is, without question, alluring.

"Imagine," she coos in the center of the warm fire-lit room. "Just go ahead and imagine yourself naked." Long-fingered hands float up from her sides. Her chin tilts upward and she exudes a kind of sexual energy that makes me sure that everyone in the room is envisioning Kate, rather than themselves, naked.

"You are naked," says beautiful Kate and it may have

been too many Champagne cocktails or the midnight hour but suddenly I want to cry. I understand that this reaction comes from the often intangible allure that other women might possibly command—with larger breasts or darker hair, with less innate intensity or more patience—over my husband. It doesn't matter that I once kissed Kate while dancing in her Music Club living room. I sit on the couch in the middle of the party and I want to cry.

"You are *fully* naked." Kate, as good as naked, aligns herself with the side of a feigned bathtub. She raises a demure leg over its porcelain edge. "Not a stitch of clothing, nothing to defend yourself. You are naked as a jay! And you are going to *settle*"—alarm steals into her voice and she becomes slightly unhinged, a sexily panicked, pallid beauty who isn't entirely conscious of the draw she exerts. I want to understand, badly, what it is about my good friend that feels so eerily powerful when she says, "Do you want, do you really *want,* to sink down into a tub of someone else's chilled crap?"

Some among us are swayed and there are calls (I hear only men) of "Whoa, she's right," and "Fuuck!" and "The puke, man! You gotta choose the puke!"

So it is—with the lyrical cadence in her voice, with her pretty jawline, her implicit nudity, with her graceful hands settling on the sides of an imaginary bathtub—that Kate succeeds in convincing enough of my guests to vote against my choice, to vote that sticking your head into a bag of vomit is a better choice than taking a bath in shit.

———

Which is why, in part, it feels safer to sit on my couch— nowhere close to tears—with my friend Maeve. I love

Maeve. I consider her a close friend even though she is sixty years old, my parents' neighbor, my little sister Ellis's erstwhile Girl Scout leader. Maeve is a breast cancer survivor and our real estate agent. She is a contradiction who was born in Arkansas where she was shuttled in and out of six different foster homes but has lived for decades in a multi-million dollar home in affluent Atherton. Maeve is a bottle-blond pistol who wears pancake makeup to the gym, to her ballet class, and to the Giants games she attends religiously. I love her because she laughs easily in great happy gusts. She'll tell you that you need a pair of ivy topiaries to "finish your foyer" just before telling you to "quit thinking with your twat."

As in, "That is exactly what happens when you think with your twat."

This is Maeve's response when I confide what has begun to seem like paranoia: That everyone is having affairs, that parents are scientifically proven to have loads of affairs in their late thirties and early forties once the kids are making fewer demands and couples have drifted apart or have gotten bored and testy and resentful and *jealous*.

Maeve sees that I am concerned. She nods slowly. This nod might be my mother's, except for how Maeve cants her puffy blond head and squints, something tough entering her southern-born features.

"Let me ask you something." She brings a plump knee under her to face where I sit close on the couch. "Do you know why men are like linoleum?"

I shake my head, smiling as we move further from my mother's territory.

"Lay 'em right the first time and you can walk all over 'em."

I laugh, amused as much by Maeve's burst of laughter as her joke.

"That's just a joke," she states the obvious. "But I'm telling it to you because there's truth in it. You're sitting here thinking this idea of having an affair is something new. You're thinking it has to do with babies getting older."

"Yes."

She dismisses this notion with a wave of her well-manicured hand. "Affairs don't have to do with that. Listen to me. Sure the kids are hard. Believe me—they don't get any easier. But you have to take care of the linoleum. You have to sweep it and scrub it and polish it. Not just sex. Not so you can walk all over your husband. That was a joke." She pauses. "But you really do have to work at it."

I nod.

"Arthur has complete confidence in our relationship."

I smile at mention of the hoary-bearded soft-spoken man who has spent all these decades devoted to brash Maeve. "I love Arthur," I say.

"I do too." She softens. "But we've fallen down before. Arthur and I. We sure have. But we get back up. Arthur and I work hard. Which is not a new idea!"

Laying a hand on my forearm, she lowers her voice, smiling at the memory she's about to share. "In Italy last summer we had this dinner party. There's a doctor in the village who is crazy for me. I mean just crazy for me. This man is flirting with me all night long," and when Maeve's hand comes coquettishly to her throat I see the slapdash beauty the Italian doctor would have fallen for. "I was sure Arthur hadn't noticed. He isn't the jealous type. He's really just not the type to notice. Everyone left and do you know what Arthur says to me? He says, 'Honey, the man's crazy for you,' and I said, 'Arthur, I know. He is just crazy for me.' But the important thing here is that once Arthur said it, all the sexual tension was out in the open. You've communicated it. That takes the sting out. And the temptation." Her brows come together as though she's remembering something important. "Because you have to keep flirting."

I fight the temptation to interrupt and agree that yes, flirting is important . . . to feel attractive and appreciated and intelligent. Flirting is fun. I like to flirt. But flirting seems suddenly dangerous. I voice none of this because Maeve has more to say.

"I went back to Italy by myself that fall."

I pull up an incongruous image of Maeve in a pink ballet leotard standing alone on the sunny loggia of the small Italian villa she and Arthur live for.

"I invited people up from the village for dinner. The man who's crazy for me came and I mean with his *mother*. Everyone knows him, all these people up from the village because he's the doctor. He's a good doctor. Of course, the two of us were the only ones who could speak English. He looks at me right in the middle of dinner. He says, 'I will meet you here tomorrow afternoon and we will make love for a week.'" Maeve's laughter is an infectious braying. "Everyone looked at me because I was shocked. *Shocked!* I said to Giancarlo, 'This is not an appropriate topic to discuss at the moment.' But I tell you, if I had said, 'You come on over tomorrow afternoon,' things would have been different.

"The point is that I told Arthur the very next day on the phone. We laughed and laughed. He really has complete confidence in our relationship. Confidence and trust. You have to laugh at these things. And communicate. You can flirt a little, that's fine, but you have to communicate and you have to laugh. At all these people who are just crazy for you."

I smile at Maeve. I think of her with Arthur and Giancarlo at some rustic Italian dinner table and I feel better.

————

So much better that, without thinking it through, I take Maeve's advice that very Friday.

Bill and I grab dinner in Palo Alto before walking around the corner to Watercourse Way.

My mom and Ellis and I have been patrons of the WW— an Asian-inspired spa—since I was old enough to get a massage at what . . . fourteen? Not until recently, though, have I understood why anyone would ever say yes when they ask during the massage booking if you'd care to spend the hour before your appointment in one of their nine tub rooms.

I may love sensation, but I am not a Jacuzzi person. The chlorine fumes make me think the whole experience is more toxic than relaxing and I get way too hot. Plus Ellis contracted hot tub folliculitis (that's really what it's called) a decade ago. The idea that a warren of indoor hot tubs exists in downtown Palo Alto for people to pop in and out of hourly seems totally repugnant.

"But, whoa," my friend Todd said a couple of years ago when I acted like he was some kind of sicko for "tubbing" there. "You don't go for the hot tub."

"You don't?" I was missing something.

"No." He looked at me like I was an idiot. "There's a *bed* in the room. The rooms are *nice*. You feel like you're in Morocco or Japan or India, depending on the room. You rent the room for an hour and you go *fuck*."

"Noo," I breathed, delighted by everything except not having understood before now.

Todd then introduced the term Bill and I would make ample use of, Watercourse Way becoming a second home. "Why else," asked Todd, "do you think they call it 'Soak 'n' Poke'?"

So here are Bill and I in "One Pine," a room lined with wood that might have come from the inside of Napa Valley wine barrels or the hull of a Japanese sailing vessel. We've had good sex so blasé Bill is happily floating around in the petri tub while I sit cross-legged on the taut-linened mattress, not so much as a toe near the water.

"Just out of curiosity," I lob through the soothing air they scent with some kind of balsam or essential oils or something. "Of all the women we know," I ask an unsuspecting Bill, "who would you want to fuck?"

My husband looks at me like I just scooped up a handful of the water I'm convinced is foul and slurped it down. He stands up in the waist-deep tub as though rising will help him understand what I've said. "What kind of a question is that?"

"It's not a bad one. Kate? How about Kate?"

Bill's surprise becomes humored and indulgent confusion. "I like Kate. Kate's great. She's really thoughtful."

And my heart sinks. This utterly normal response should reassure. Bill is entirely unruffled, he's not stammering or red-in-the-face or in any way suspicious looking.

When I'm quiet he's kind enough to say, "Are you really worried about this? Are you serious with that question?"

"Yes! It's weird. Lately. Because of what my mom said. And because I keep hearing about all these people having affairs. We are so happy, you and I. We're just so lucky."

"We are. You're right."

"I don't know why I'm worried." I'm worried because the enormous amount of sexual energy between us feels so potent and that potency feels well within our control, but what if it weren't? What if it spilled over or something?

"There's nothing for you to worry about." He stepped closer but was still a solid ten feet away. "Really."

"I'm not worried that you're actually going to have an affair and leave me." I'm worried because the mere idea of Bill finding another woman more alluring or attractive or intelligent is devastating.

"Good. You don't need to."

"I don't know what it is." But I wonder if this particular sensitivity comes from feeling like the two of us are both happier sexually but also more socially engaged than we ever have been. I wonder if the renaissance of my flirtatious and fun-loving prekids self has meant becoming more aware of the sexual currents running through so much social interaction. This particular focus on Kate? Probably from the fact that I myself love to be with Kate. I mean, my God, I *kissed* Kate. I love running into her at school. I look forward to our drinking wine together on the loggia where we talk so easily about music and our families and our lives.

Or maybe this is simple age-old jealousy, the insecurity that dates back to grade school when a girlfriend seems prettier, happier, better loved by the boy you have a crush on. "I don't know," I say to Bill. Then, because I want more from him I say, "But it's bothering me."

"Well . . ."

"Well, what? You don't want to fuck Kate?"

"No." He looks me right in the eye. "I do not want to fuck Kate."

"That's good."

"Yeah. But I guess if you're worried about this stuff then it's good to get it out in the open."

And I'm a little surprised by how much Bill sounds like Maeve.

"You can diffuse a lot of stuff," he says, "by talking about it. By communicating."

Isn't that exactly what Maeve had said?

"Isn't that the key?" he continues. "Getting it out there?"

I nod, pleased that he's engaging me, even if he does seem to be channeling our real estate agent. He's taking my concerns seriously and his response is reassuring. I sit feeling uncommonly young, little even, naked and wanting to move closer to his body even though it's interesting—poignant—to have such an intimate conversation while remaining across the room from each other.

"After all," says Bill, "people flirt."

It's like Maeve called the guy and prepped him.

"Well," Bill qualifies, "I don't flirt that much."

I consider this, and nod.

"You don't either. Not really . . ." Now Bill is the one who considers. "Not that much anyway."

"No," I confirm, glad he thinks so because I like to flirt as much as the next woman.

"We," says Bill, making me smile with how he's unconsciously jiggling his balls there in the warm water, "are really lucky."

He states it simply and I want to cry—not on my cocktail

couch where I'm threatened by a close friend's allure—but because we *are* so lucky. I smile on the white-sheeted bed. I allow myself the indulgent but convincing thought that what I really need to do is trust this man.

Then it's like he's reading my mind, not Maeve's.

"You just need to trust me," he says. And with this my husband sinks contentedly into the disgusting water to float around some more.

CHAPTER 20

Into the Sunset

B ut so you finally regain enough energy—as a couple— to get back to the discussion of high concepts. Like trust. Or compatibility. Or self-fulfillment. You can actually begin and sustain and finish a conversation about deceit or pleasure or responsibility. Because the kids are older. The kids fix their own snacks now and ride bikes to each other's houses for playdates, all of which creates brief oases of time when the two of you can hang out together on the loggia or sit on the couch or lean against a kitchen counter and talk.

And parents appreciate these moments in ways that childless couples might not! Long ago you two had sex that created new people who taxed your relationship and your sex life, but you've come through it mostly unscathed! There against the kitchen counter a mom can let her saggy stomach relax; she can say pretty much anything that occurs to her; she doesn't have to worry about how her hair's looking. All because she's talking to a man who remembers her pre-babies belly and appreciates the sacrifice of her figure. Her husband has heard her say some crazy things, and he's surely seen her in *much* less flattering states . . . and he loves her anyway. There on the living room couch a dad can slide over to sit with his back to his wife, who knows him well enough to understand that this means he wants his neck rubbed. And even though his wife is dead tired, she rubs his neck anyway.

Your discussion of intimacy or anxiety or integrity will then be interrupted by a kid wailing in the next room and you might band together momentarily against that child, but by then a different child will also need you or you will decide to do the dishes after all or that someone needs homework help or you'll realize it's somehow gotten to be bedtime.

But imagine there's no interruption. Imagine a certain writer coming through the door and asking this couple if they have any final thoughts on sex and parenting. How is their marriage inflected by children? Does parenting mean increased richness and trust and familiarity and therefore better sex? Or has parenting pretty much spelled disaster in the bedroom?

Responses to these questions just might look something like this:

————

Katherine and Paul L. (Remember the Zing Cream on his popsicle? Remember his penis hanging out of his pajamas?) hadn't been away alone, without their three kids, for over

fourteen months. The romantic weekend they were supposed to spend in Monterey? Foiled by lice in one darling
towhead, which meant forty-eight hours of laundering and
vacuuming and shampooing five heads with toxic liquids
instead of all the fucking that Katherine and Paul had
planned for the sunny deck of the secluded cliff house.

When that devastation was followed by two successive
nights of tears (Katherine's—successive nights of children's
tears being the norm), consolation reservations were made
by sensitive and caring Paul for a night at a swanky hotel in
the city.

Armpits were shaved, brows were waxed, a much-needed
pedicure was had. Lingerie was snatched and shoved into
the overnight bag while two-year-old Matthew clung to his
mother's leg saying "Uppy! Uppy!" which had ceased to be
cute months ago. Notes were scribbled for the brother who
had finally returned Katherine's call after having planned
to absolutely say no to the proposition he sensed was coming, but whose sister sounded so totally desperate that
Jamie had said, shit all right, okay, he'd spend the following
Saturday night with his niece and nephews.

One long week and a giddy forty-minute car ride later,
Paul and Katherine found themselves entering the city
where they had lived as newlyweds. They loved the city. In
truth, though, Paul and Katherine were feeling like newlyweds not because they had lived in the city just after they
were married, but because their youngest child was two,
which made any moment away feel like a honeymoon.
Katherine hadn't needed to explain her words when the
Volvo, its car seats blissfully empty, crested Potrero Hill and
the city lay before them and she had said, "I love this."

In the echoing garage, the newlywed vibe built when

Paul lifted the overnight bag from his wife's shoulder. Paul was able to lift the overnight bag from his wife's shoulder because Paul's arms were not full of the toddler who insisted on being carried by his father. And don't think Katherine's brows didn't rise at this attention, her comment, "Chivalry appears to be alive and well," garnering a lowered-voice promise from Paul who said, "Chivalry's not the only thing that's alive and well."

Down the block they went, up the stairs and into the miraculously hushed lobby of the swanky hotel.

"Super," the blond twenty-something receptionist was saying, "I have an imprint of your card and, let's see . . . uh-huh, looks like we have your . . . mailing address on file . . ." Across the counter came the credit card and a fancy receipt on some kind of card stock.

But Paul was eyeing the keys. As the receptionist typed, paused, typed some more, Paul noted that this hotel had gone back to metal keys with encoded magnetic strips. Metal keys, thought Paul, felt nice in the hand. Paul nodded his head almost imperceptibly while thinking that a key wasn't the only thing that would feel nice in the hand.

The receptionist leaned close to the computer screen. She stood up again typed rapidly. She stared some more.

Paul eased over to stand with his body against Katherine's, which was making him more aroused and therefore more creative with the sexual innuendo that had become a kind of kid-proof parlance between himself and Katherine, a kind of game but also—Paul liked to think—a minor sort of art form. Paul was also, though, becoming more sentimental. It seemed comforting and significant to him that the hotel industry had come full circle from notched metal keys to programmable plastic cards then back to electronically encoded keys that felt good in the hand, this cycle having completed itself during the fifteen years—fifteen years!—in which he'd known his wife.

"Now if you'll allow me," the receptionist looked suddenly up, "to tell you about our outstanding amenities!"

At which Paul said into his wife's ear, "I'll show *you* amenities."

The receptionist swung her glance down a hallway, pretending not to register Paul's comment as she raised an open hand to indicate world-class spa and exercise facilities.

Katherine gazed down the hallway, less to please the receptionist than to indulge herself in all that was connoted by "world-class spa." The idea was enough. There would be no time for facials. Still, Katherine envisioned herself alone—with not one single child—reclining in a steam bath. Katherine imagined herself lying by herself in a sauna. Katherine saw herself sipping aromatherapeutic tea while waiting for her massage therapist to retrieve her from a quiet low-lit lounge, at which idea (the masseur entering her fantasy was of course uncommonly attractive) a euphoric Katherine reached a sly palm to cup her husband's ass cheek and give it a nice upward-lifting squeeze.

"The hotel also offers a wide variety of exercise classes and personal training." At which Paul flexed his bicep against Katherine's bicep in a kind of mating dance that was necessary because this annoying woman couldn't see that Katherine and Paul—expected back at home by ten the next morning—wanted nothing more than the keys.

"Our professional fitness staff is unparalleled," this useless information blending into the non sequitous, "Were you considering a meal here at the hotel?"

And because Katherine thought her husband might say, "Oh, I'm gonna have a *meal*"—which Katherine would find totally funny despite the image of her husband's head between her legs—she lied and said, "We've made reservations already, thanks."

After which Paul was certain that the keys would come across the high counter.

But the receptionist smiled an unexpected little Cheshire smile that Paul the innuendoist couldn't help but appreciate, his arm snaking around his wife's shoulder, his hand kneading her arm. "You two," the receptionist said, "have chosen a wonderful time to visit."

"That right?" Paul managing to freight the simple question, his hand moving down his wife's back.

"It's Coit month here at the hotel."

"It's what?" Katherine guffawed.

"You know, honey," said Paul with the straightest of faces. "Coit. The tower."

"Yes," the receptionist was all enthusiasm. "With self-guided tours and historical information available at the concierge. It's one of San Francisco's most prominent landmarks. If—"

"You know." Paul pressed into the counter. His voice was kind, its tenor and warmth convincing this woman that she had done an exceptional job of informing her clientele, but that he needed to explain something almost intimate to her.

"This all sounds outstanding." He had taken up Katherine's hand and was rubbing her palm with his thumb and it felt really good and Katherine moved closer to him. "It all sounds great. But we've got three kids at home."

Which, from the look on her young face, meant nothing to the receptionist.

"We have nineteen hours." Paul was earnest. "We're only going to be climbing one tower."

From Katherine, laughter.

From the receptionist, silence.

"If you really want to make our stay memorable"—here was sweet Paul giving this stranger the opportunity to succeed—"you will pass me those keys."

———

Shelly T. (Remember the progressive Palo Alto preschool? Remember Shelly's bastard husband who left eight-weeks pregnant Shelly for another woman? Remember handsome single Greg and the seventh hole?). Well Shelly T. remarried an amazing man named James a number of years after the birth of her first child, Amanda, and has been very happy with her second husband.

Shelly T. has the kind of relationship with her down-to-earth photographer husband, James, that allows the two of them, Shelly and James, to sometimes unite against their kids in a slightly adversarial way when their now adolescent children (they had gone on to give Amanda a brother and a sister) were acting like assholes.

It was James, in fact, who was there at the kitchen table—Shelly and James each with a cup of coffee, he with the paper, she with her laptop—when college freshman Amanda sent her mother a certain emotion-evoking email.

"Oh hey." Shelly sounded pleased. "Amanda sent something."

"Good." James glanced up from the paper, conveying pleasure at Amanda having sent something because Amanda and her mother were uncommonly close and it had been hard this fall what with Shelly's peri-menopausal craziness

(peri-menopausal craziness at only forty-six!) being exacer-
bated by her daughter's leaving. Contact from Amanda was
good. Contact from Amanda had been somewhat rare and
was valued by both James and Shelly.

This morning, however, Amanda's often effusive and typically longish missive was replaced with a single line: "You
have got to see this!!!! Hilarious!!!!!!!!" followed by a link.

Back to his paper, James was not overly distracted by the
faint, peppy audio of whatever his wife was watching.

Until Shelly shook her head, made a clicking noise with
her tongue. "Unbelievable."

James lowered his paper. "What."

"Look at what Amanda sent me."

The clip she loaded while turning the laptop to face her
husband was the exact kind of genius that has made
YouTube such a force. The clip was a mock JCPenney adver-
tisement for "Mom Jeans." In and out of minivans cavorted
pairs and trios of paunchy mothers whose light denim
jeans practically reached their ribs. The pants' selling points
included their (preposterous) nine-inch zipper, the (illogical) lack of pockets that showcased the enormous moon-
shaped derriere of a squatting mom, the availability of
an elastic waistband, and a hokey patchwork vest that any
lucky mother would receive with the purchase of any
"Mom Jeans." Had she not been forty-six and peri-
menopausal and disappointed that a heartfelt letter from
her daughter was not forthcoming, Shelly might have been
amused.

Instead she said to James, "That little shit!"

And here's the excellent thing. Because Shelly and James
had been together for thirteen years, there was no doubt in

either of their minds that James revered his wife's body. James had in fact made more mention of Shelly's legs and ass than any other part of her body. Which did not lead Shelly to believe that he didn't love the rest of her body because there was plenty of attention paid to her breasts and arms and back too. Shelly was convinced, rightly or wrongly, that her husband was crazy about her peri-menopausal body in general and her peri-menopausal ass and legs in particular.

So what did this smart husband do to reassure his wife that their daughter's e-mail shouldn't be taken as an insult? How did he assure her that she had nothing in common with the fat-bottomed, pot-bellied, fluffy-haired women in the mildly offensive (but also pretty funny) spoof? James asked Shelly to stand up.

"No." Shelly laughed. "That's ridiculous."

"Seriously. You're wearing jeans. Stand up."

And Shelly wasn't wearing just any jeans. Shelly was wearing a pair of James's jeans. This might have been depressing, wearing more or less the same size jeans as your husband. But these were worn and faded 501s that made both Shelly and James feel good. James, discerning man, had recently said that he liked these jeans on her better than the expensive Lucky Brand ones she had brought home after a dispiriting visit to the shopping center. On Shelly, James's 501s were baggy in all the right places. They were soft and classic in a way that made both Shelly and James feel younger, as opposed to the fashionable but too-low-waisted Lucky Brand jeans that James liked well enough, but that make Shelly feel—paradoxically—old.

Shelly stood before her husband.

James didn't rise. He didn't put a move on her (though his support and encouragement was foreplay, his kitchen-table attentions contributed to the good sex these seasoned lovers would have later). James sat. He looked at his wife's body. He said, "Those jeans are good, Shell. You look good."

She looked down at the jeans. "They are good, aren't they?" She fingered the worn seam running down her thigh then looked to her husband. "You know what?"

"What?"

"This . . ." And she paused, James unsure if "this" referred to the clip Amanda had sent or the way he was looking at her or what. "This," she said again as she bent to kiss him on the mouth, "makes me miss Amanda a whole lot less."

———

John and Allison R. (Remember them? He can sense when she's ovulating? They occasionally shave her pubes over a towel they spread out on their bed?) were getting ready for date night.

Allison stepped out of the shower, saw her reflection next to her husband's in the mirror where John was brushing his teeth.

"Shoot!" she said.

Her husband rinsed. "What?"

"I am fat!"

At which John turned to wife and said, "You just noticed?"

(Which sounds like he's being critical—but he's not, which is the real point of the story.)

When John said, "You just noticed?" Allison laughed a genuinely amused, relieved, and totally appreciative laugh.

Because John honestly doesn't care that his wife is carrying an extra dozen pounds (of "baby fat," the "baby" now in first grade). John likes pressing his hands into ass cheeks that are fuller and firmer than they used to be and John likes the way the extra weight makes his wife look younger than some of the skinnier moms at school who are starting to look a little . . . weathered.

What John appreciates is that his wife gets it when he sidles up to her at a party and gives her a certain look that says that she's ovulating—a fact that disorganized, carefree Allison would *never* know on her own—and that they both might enjoy a couples' jaunt to the bathroom.

As for Allison, she finds it deeply satisfying that John is more turned on by shaving off her public hair than the idea of her returning to a size six. Allison is moved by the fact that her husband supports her choice to nap rather than spend hours in the salon, hence the salt-and-pepper hair that work for both of them.

Allison was perceptive enough recently to appreciate John's unconditional love when a special evening rolled around and she wanted to borrow a fabulous wrap dress from a friend then decided it might look a tad better with Spanx underneath. Well, John thought it was crazy that she would want to wear a *girdle* (his word) because a *girdle* was totally unnecessary and she looked great without it. Allison wanted to give John a little sense of the difference and sensitive John managed his reaction perfectly, deliberating a good long while before agreeing that just *maybe* the Spanx weren't a terrible idea.

And over the years she and John had fought enough and laughed enough and had developed enough trust and familiarity for her to know that he would laugh—which he did—when she told him her favorite part of the evening during the drive home. What was best about the evening, according to Allison, was the fact that her pubes had grown out to such a length that they kind of stuck out through the "pee-hole" (her word) in the "girdle" (his word). She explained that it had actually felt really nice all night, while she was walking around the party, with her little brush of pubes sweeping against her thighs. Allison was pretty sure he'd have to "have his way with her" once she worked her way out of the Spanx that John had thought at first were such a bad idea but that, in the end, might well have worked out in his favor.

———

Kendall N. (Remember the hip Manhattan loft and the single-kid plan? Remember the snapped condom?) tucked six-year-old Thayer into the top bed of the IKEA bunks, Thayer's little accidental brother, Leo, already fast asleep below him.

And Kendall did not take for granted the fact that the boys had settled down easily. Kendall very much appreciated their cooperation because she was midcycle, which meant ovulation and the increased interest in sex that both she and Rob had identified. (Had you approached Rob Nichols—one of four boys—on his wedding night and told him that he would become this familiar with his bride's hormonal fluctuations he would have said you were crazy.)

There would be no lingerie involved in this midcycle romp. Kendall wasn't a fan. There wouldn't be a vibrator either, given that Kendall hadn't gotten around to buying the Magic Wand a girlfriend told her she simply could not do without.

But no matter. Because Kendall and Rob had been together for a long time.

Kendall and Rob had developed a relatively ample repertoire that meant (as opposed to earlier in their relationship) that pretty much every time they had sex, Kendall had an orgasm. There was a certain missionary-style thing where she sort of rocked slowly against him . . . worked every time! There was good old-fashioned cunnilingus that Rob had gotten down to a total science and there was a new trick with him behind while Kendall engaged in a little digital stimulation, a recent favorite. There had even been a handful of times in the past month or so—these not easily replicable for whatever reason—when Kendall had had two orgasms!

"Wow," she had said afterward, Rob lying open-mouthed and closed-eyed beside her. "That was . . . different."

"No shit," he said.

"Not just that." She whapped his chest with the back of her hand. "It was like . . . something in there was . . . higher up."

He rolled to face her, smiling because this sounded odd.

"Inside of me. Some part of me, not you. I don't know, like my cervix or something." This being the kind of thing Kendall could say to her husband only now, after he had impregnated her and seen her give birth and had come to understand menstrual minutia and had become far more familiar with Kendall's genital geography than she would ever be. "I think," she mused, "it must have to do with my cycle."

"Is that . . . good or bad?"

"It's not good or bad," she said. "It's just . . . interesting."

Those second orgasms, though? That was clearly good. That was new and exciting and made both Rob and Kendall feel like monogamy wasn't a dead end after all.

This thought was further affirmed some weeks later when Rob discovered that sucking hard on Kendall's neck—an old-school hickey! something they'd never tried before!—was inexplicably arousing for both of them. Further affirmation that long-term monogamy promised good stuff was Kendall's discovery that Rob actually had a better orgasm if she could manage to reach around (or under or over) to sort of squeeze his scrotum when the time came.

Or how about when Kendall's girlfriend had said, "The whole G-spot thing is no myth. Daniel can totally find mine." Well, Kendall and Rob hadn't gone in for any G-spot exploration, but Kendall was inspired to comment to Rob that "apparently Daniel has no trouble finding Lisa's G-spot." Which led to some light research on Rob's part (one of the Internet's finest applications). Research was followed by laughter that night in bed when Rob's elbow was momentarily but pretty awkwardly twisted when Kendall rolled over unexpectedly just as he was getting into research-recommended position, the two of them more than a little elated to confirm eight minutes later that the G-spot was, in fact, a real thing. Turned out that Kendall's orgasms lasted longer and were far more intense with that kind of stimulation! Turned out, this discovery made a couple of weeks later, that Rob's dick was just as good at finding the G-spot as his finger! The result: an amazing series of simultaneous orgasms that seemed to elevate sex to a new, more emotional and meaningful plane.

After one such simultaneously orgasmic experience Kendall rolled over to Rob, who was drifting off. "You know?" she poked his ribs. "I couldn't do all this with just anybody."

Which brought Rob far enough out of his postcoital stupor to say, "Well that's good to hear."

But what his wife meant was that she wouldn't want to teach anybody else about her G-spot (she actually had no idea where it was or what exactly Rob was doing down there). She couldn't imagine having to tell someone that her nipples were really sensitive, which was a good thing, or that she generally liked to start things out with her on top where her fingertips had good access to her important parts. Kendall didn't feel the need, though, to explain any of this to Rob. He was sleepy. He was a really good dad and a really good husband and wow, really a very good lover, especially lately. So she liked the idea of him being able to drift off. She rolled over onto her side. With her butt pressed up against her husband's naked hip all Kendall said was, "You know what I mean."

Kimberly locked the Private Time door while Bill took a leak.

Naked, Bill sprawled on the bed that no one ever made because their newlywed "Division of Labor" plan (bedmaking and garbage being Bill's sole items) went to shit when the kids were born and a made bed was no longer a priority.

Kimberly dug in the bottom drawer of the bedside table and extracted her Magic Wand. Leaning forward, one hand braced on the bedside table, she threaded the other

arm between the wall and the headboard where she had
become adept at plugging her accoutrement into a socket
she could not see.

She jabbed around. She listened to the little prongs
scrape the wall (not worried about the paint because this
part of the wall was hidden by the bed; also not worried because both she and Bill would think it was funny—a source
of pride—if the bedroom furniture were rearranged and a
scratched-up wall were revealed as a kind of testament to
Private Time).

She leaned further forward, the vibrator cord now tangled in the lamp cord.

Head tucked slightly down as she stretched, Kimberly
was given a view of her body. Small boobs. Really tiny
boobs. And not attractive from this angle. Kind of triangu-
lar. Pointy, which Kimberly didn't find attractive in breasts.
Another aspect that made boobs less attractive were nipple
hairs. Like the one that had just become visible at her left
nipple, her left boob already at a barely perceptible disad-
vantage, her left boob being a fraction smaller than her
right. She squinted at her sorry boobs thinking with rue
that those very boobs had been a D-cup (!) during much of
the almost six years she had spent nursing her three
children. She wondered—the plug scraping against the
wall, she muttering a lightweight "fuuuck!"—if her big
boobs had been good for Bill, who liked large breasts well
enough, or if six years of such big boobs was actually not-
so-good in that he had gotten a taste of what he would
never, for the rest of his life, have again.

Below the sad boobs? Her tummy. Now her tummy
looked all right when she was standing up (good genes).
But when she leaned over like this her stomach hung like

an empty sack. She sucked it in and it looked better. Sort of. Wrinkly though, like an old lady's, which is never good.

So she straightened up some, which was awkward for the cord business (though she finally found the slots). Straightening took care of the saggy tummy, but what then became visible was the line of odd puckery scars, each shaped like a deformed penny from where she had "spit" the outdated silk sutures her eighty-year-old obstetrician had used on the internal incision of her first C-section (The black spiky sutures had worked their way up through fascia then epidermis where they first created a mysterious little welt, then a scabby sore before each little loop-tied stitch could actually be plucked out by a trusty nurse-practitioner sister who was gleefully fascinated by the whole disgusting phenomenon.). Below the row of penny scars ran the lumpy bumpy flesh that overlaid scar tissue. The scar tissue was so lumpy and bumpy, in fact, that it was hard for her to see the dark red line of the C-section scar that ran from one side of her lower abdomen all the way to the other.

Her vibrator mission accomplished, she straightened up further. With hands pressing her tummy in as far as it could go, she examined a red bump that looked suspiciously like another spit suture—but now? nine years later? could that be possible?!

When she noticed that naked Bill was watching her.

"What." She dropped her hands to her sides, flushed in a mostly good way because her husband had been watching her, which was nice, but his watching was also a little disconcerting given that she had taken her hands from her belly and had been standing there scowling, trying to pluck the pesky hair from her left nipple when she noticed he was staring at her. She repeated, "What."

But Bill smiled. "Nothing."

"What?"

He reached out a lazy arm. He ran a finger along the lumpy bumpy dark red line. "I was looking at your scar."

It was not an attractive one. It was dark and bulgy and longer than it should have been.

"It's nice," he said and she believed him. "It's crazy."

"What's crazy."

"That it's kind of a big deal. I mean . . . for what it is. But that really, you can hardly even see it."

The End:
A Conclusion (of Sorts)

Yesterday was one of those days. Not that "one of those days" feels very different from any other day for your average mom of youngish children. I woke up at four-thirty in the morning because my best hours promised to be those in which I was writing. By six-thirty I was at the ice-skating rink with Hannah, who practices before school twice a week. Eight saw me at the always-harried elementary school drop-off; eight-thirty racing back home for Xavier's forgotten seed pod for sharing; eight-forty-five hustling through the bright green door of his beloved nursery school. With all three of my children in other people's care for a blissful two hours I stole to the café down the hill from the nursery school where I wrote for another two hours, lost track of time, and had to sprint back up with my computer bag wonky over one shoulder, my handbag over the other, and a totally ill-planned, spilling, but completely indispensable cappuccino in my outstretched grip. Any parent can imagine how the day went from there.

The afternoon, though, felt different from any other. The afternoon was haunted by a conversation. It wasn't a new warning from my mother or seven-year-old Hannah's cemetery-inspired query as to "why anybody would ever want their body buried *in the ground*?" It wasn't nine-year-old Lucas's announcement as I hugged him good-bye that the major diorama book report we hadn't started yet was due tomorrow.

The conversation that echoed through nursery school pickup and elementary school pickup, the drive to San Mateo for the pitching clinic, and the race back for soccer practice took place during the precious two hours I had spent writing at the café.

My friend Maria had popped in for a cup of tea after the yoga class she had just finished with her friend Stephanie.

"So, wow," Stephanie smiled as they propped their rolled mats against their chairs and agreed to sit for a minute. "*Hump! True Tales of . . . ?*"

"*Sex After Kids,*" I said with a kind of glee.

"Isn't that great?" said Maria, whose pride in my endeavor was totally heartwarming.

Stephanie narrowed her eyes as though she worked for a local venture capital firm and was considering an investment of millions. "Who's your target audience?"

"Parents," I said. "Moms mostly. But dads too."

"And how old are your kids?" Stephanie now appeared to want a handle on how germane the book was for her personally.

"Five, seven, and nine." I marveled at how old they sounded, Xavier having just celebrated a birthday.

"Mmm-hmm." Here Stephanie and Maria exchanged knowing glances that perplexed me. Maria, whose daughter was thirteen, explained, "Stephanie's daughter goes to school with Louisa."

"See," said Stephanie. "I think it's a whole lot trickier when your kids get older. I mean, when my kids were your kids' ages they didn't really get it. By twelve . . . thirteen it's a different ball game."

I was struck by this unforeseen reality. I was astounded as always by the myopia that prevents me from imagining the reality of parenting kids who are so much as a day older than mine. As I processed Stephanie's comment, I wondered as I sometimes do if my kids "got it." Sure Bill and I had led them through the mechanics of reproduction on practically the same day we instituted Private Time, but just the other evening inquisitive Hannah indicated that they had made no connection between intercourse and recreation. "What do you guys *do* during Private Time?" she asked. "We chat," I answered. "I get a backrub if I'm lucky," which seemed to entirely satisfy her.

"When our kids were little"—Stephanie set down her green tea—"we could just . . . go about things. Now that they've put the pieces together, the house can feel . . . complicated."

I imagined Bill and me making out in the kitchen or on the living-room couch while our teen-age kids slouched morosely (no longer skipping or tumbling) around us. I imagined us heading upstairs after announcing Private Time to thirteen-, fifteen- and seventeen-year-olds, who would be totally grossed out.

"Oh, yeah," said Maria, who was further alarming me with the slow and foreboding nod of her head. She smiled, half-teasing when she said, "Denial has to be the best approach to sex and teens."

"Absolutely!" Stephanie laughed. "Which is why the all-girls' school is such a good call."

I thought of how I felt no over whelming need to send Hannah to the all-girls' school Maria's and Stephanie's daughters attended, even though it happened to be my alma mater. With the start Bill and I had gotten off to, denial didn't seem like an option. Besides which, I actually like to think about my kids having fulfilling sex lives when they're adults. I welcome the idea of communicating about these issues along the way. It just hadn't occurred to me that parenting adolescents might prove stickier than shepherding my curious—but content and unsavvy—elementary-schoolers. My God, could living with glowering teens actually prove worse for our sex life than the dark days of parenting very young children?

I wanted to believe—perhaps naïvely—that the open lines of communication I had worked hard to establish would allow me to maintain the kind of harmonious and communicative relationships with my teenagers that a couple of my friends seem to enjoy with theirs. I reassured myself that even if my adolescents made life complicated with moodiness and self-absorption and hormone gluts, surely they'd be out of the house more. They'd padlock their churlish selves in their bedrooms or come up with more inventive ways to leave Bill and me ample time for what we now accomplish during officially sanctioned Private Time hours.

"Looks like you'll have to write a sequel!" said Stephanie

cheerily as she and Maria stood, gathering their mats and their teas.

"Yeah," I said, managing a wave as they banged out the café door.

My preoccupation, though, lasted no more than the duration of my aforementioned sprint up the hill to Xavier's school. The little lug was sprawled on the circle-time carpet, parents stepping over and around his splayed body while he insisted that he needed to be carried to the car. "I'm *soooo* tired. From all the swinging and swinging on the swings." He groaned. "I'm so tired I can't move a bone." Xavier's unwieldiness was followed by the unparalleled chaos of minimum-day elementary pickup followed by baseball practice, soccer practice, and a late-afternoon stop by the market, all of which precluded further reflection.

As we filed into the house around five, though (Bill traveling for work in Paris, of all cities), the specter of adolescence returned. Xavier and Hannah began fighting over *Kids' Choice Awards* versus *The Naked Brothers Band* while Lucas lobbied for the totally inappropriate but occasionally daddy-sanctioned *Family Guy*. There was actual homework—an entire diorama book report—to complete, and the noxious odor I had thought was something rotting in the fridge turned out to be Lucas's cleats. It wasn't until I heard the *crack!* and *fiiizzz* of Xavier opening a Diet Coke left over from my in-laws' recent stay that I realized that my baby had not only learned to open a soda can by himself but had also thought that a Coke was a good beverage to suck down when you've just turned five.

Standing in the middle of the kitchen, I wondered what Maria and Stephanie were going through with their teens at that moment. I thought of Bill. I wished he were here to talk this over, or to simply head out for a glass of wine in the living room where I could listen to him talk about buyouts and margins for a while. Or we could discuss the latest Decemberists album or which movie he got to see (lucky bastard) on his most recent string of flights.

Right then the phone rings. It's Bill! "I was just thinking about you." I sigh into the phone.

"You were?" I can hear him smile. "That's good." He asks about Xavier's soccer and Hannah's skating. He wants me to tell Lucas that they are way ahead in their fantasy baseball league. Just as I'm about to launch into Maria and Stephanie and the possibility of adolescents cramping our newfound style, Bill says, "Can you do me a favor?"

I switch into efficient-wife mode, ready to e-mail him a document or forward a K-1 to the tax man.

"Can you," he asks, "talk to me?"

I stare at my reflection in the microwave. "What?"

I then realize it's two in the morning in Paris. I imagine Bill lying on some fancy hotel bed, a pillow mashed behind his head.

"Can you," he tries again, his voice a little lower, "talk to me?"

And I understand all at once that I am about to engage in what my college friend Caroline had raved about decades before.

"Oh my God," I say into the phone. "I can." I seize the Coke from Xavier. I swivel to hand Lucas his book report book. I dash across the room and shove the remote at Hannah whispering, "spelling words *first*, then *Naked Brothers*," before rushing out to the living room.

I flop onto the couch, breathless from racing instead of arousal. I dive in with a sultry "What are you wearing?" and cringe at the cliché. Bill, though, doesn't seem to mind. And we're off! He's murmuring stuff and I'm murmuring stuff. I'm purely indulging him for the first minute or so, but then I discover that Caroline's tried-and-true secret for maintaining long-distance relationships is seriously arousing.

"You know what I'm going to do?" I murmur into the phone. "I'm going to put my hand on my crotch." I do and I'm surprised—pleased!—at how good this feels. I tell Bill this and in far-off Paris my husband sounds like he's enjoying himself as much as I am.

"Hold on," I say, as if this is necessary. "Hold on," I repeat. "You know what I'm doing now? You know what I'm doing right now?" I speak in the breathy voice I model on Catherine Rose. "I'm going up the stairs." I take them two at a time. "This," I say to him, "is going to be goood."

There on the tiled bathroom floor, mashed into the little lockable toilet alcove with my head crunched against one wall, my knees near the toilet and the silver bomber pressed to my crotch, Bill pulls out all the stops.

My sweet husband narrates the porn playing out on the French television screen before him. Huge round breasts, perfect nipples. His mesmeric voice continues and I realize it includes pretty much just my favorite porn scenarios— sucking on big boobs, tugging on nipples, pressing round firm breasts together to fuck them with a hard cock. I begin to wonder if he's inventing it all just for me. I will later confirm what I suspect . . . that there is zero porn on his French television set. Which is so sweet!

Happily, I go along. I tell him what I'd do with those boobs, what I'd want the imagined porn star to do to mine.

He mentions an elevator in Las Vegas and I tell him that

I want him to fuck me so hard. I tell him that I want him to slap my ass (which makes me half-laugh with the phone held away because it sounds silly while I'm lying on the hard tile with Bill so far away and with the kids starting, just then, to yell at one another a floor below me).

No more than two minutes and we're both satisfied. We laugh then, the way we do after watching porn or engaging in really filthy sex-talk because it's all a little absurd. I shift to let my head settle back onto the cool tiles and laugh some more. Bill laughs. I sigh.

"That was crazy," I say.

"That was."

"But good crazy."

"Yeah." He's smiling. I can hear it. I smile too. Then Bill says, "What was it you wanted to tell me?"

I had been dying to talk with him about Maria and Stephanie and the notion that he and I might have a whole other stage of sex and parenting to negotiate. I feel far too good lying on the bathroom floor, though, to bring it up.

"It was nothing," I say as two pairs of footsteps come thundering up the stairs. I stagger upward. I smooth my skirt, preparing for heavy-duty arbitration. As I slide open the door I indulge myself in the thought that if Bill and I can discover phone sex at age thirty-seven in the middle of the crazy five o'clock hour with a nine-hour time difference and dioramas due and television squabbling at its zenith, then I think we'll be able to muddle through sex and adolescents.

"Billy," I say into the phone. "I think I have to go now."

"Sure. All right. Sounds crazy there."

"Yeah. But hey," I say softly as I hold up a menacing finger to silence our screaming children. "I'm glad you called."

USEFUL REFERENCES

Books

Angier, Natalie. *Woman: An Intimate Geography*. Boston: Houghton Mifflin, 1999.

Blank, Joani. *Good Vibrations: New Complete Guide to Vibrators*. San Francisco: Cleis, 2004.

Brizendine, Louann. *The Female Brain*. New York: Broadway Books, 2006.

Denniston, George C. *Vasectomy*. Victoria, BC, Canada: Trafford Publishing, 2002.

Dodson, Betty. *Sex for One: The Joy of Selfloving*. New York: Three Rivers Press, 1996.

Gottman, John, and Julie Schwartz Gottman. *And Baby Makes Three*. New York: Random House, 2007.

Iovine, Vicki. *The Girlfriends' Guide to Getting Your Groove Back: Loving Your Family Without Losing Your Mind*. New York: Perigee Books, 2001.

Kerner, Ian. *She Comes First: The Thinking Man's Guide to Pleasuring a Woman*. New York: Collins, 2006.

———. *He Comes Next: The Thinking Woman's Guide to Pleasuring a Man*. New York: Collins, 2008.

Locker, Sari. *The Complete Idiot's Guide to Amazing Sex*. New York: Penguin, 2003.

Wallerstein, Judith S., and Sandra Blakeslee. *The Good Marriage: How and Why Love Lasts*. Boston: Houghton Mifflin, 1995.

Winks, Cathy, and Anne Semans. *The Good Vibrations Guide to Sex*. San Francisco: Cleis, 2002.

Web sites
www.adameve.com
www.babeland.com
www.beccabrewer.com
www.goodvibes.com
www.nerve.com
www.slinkyproductions.com
www.sssh.com
www.susiebright.blogs.com

Magazines
Sweet Action (www.sweetactionmag.com)
Bust (www.bust.com)

Erotica:
Baker, Nicholson. *The Fermata*. New York: Random House, 1994.

———. *Vox. New York:* Random House, 1993.

Blue, Violet, Ed. *Best Womens Erotica 2008*. San Francisco: Cleis, 2008.

———, Ed. *Best Sex Writing 2005*. San Francisco: Cleis, 2005.

Blume, Judy. *Wifey*. New York: Berkley, 2005.

Madore, Nancy. *Enchanted: Erotic Bedtime Stories for Women*. Toronto: Spice, 2006.

Newman, Felice, and Frederique Delacoste, Eds. *Best Sex Writing 2006*. San Francisco: Cleis, 2006.

Szereto, Mitzi, Ed. *The World's Best Sex Writing 2005*. New York: Thunder's Mouth Press, 2005.

ACKNOWLEDGMENTS

This book would not have come into being without "Casey" who called from the exercise bike at the gym and told me I needed to write it. It wouldn't have happened without "Ruby" who once introduced me to a group of women as "my friend who has a lot of sex," and somehow made me feel tremendously honored by her words.

This book would have been a whole lot shorter if it weren't for my truly amazing friends "John" and "Alison," "Ellen" and "Peter," "Simone" and "Trey," "Ruby" and "John," "Liz" and "Jack," "Paul" and "Katherine," and "Kate" and "Andrew."

A handful of remarkable people shared a lot with me. To them I am indebted: "Shelly," "Eliza," "Jen," "Diane," "Elena," "Nikki" and "Ed," "Amy" and "Brian," "Laura," "Meg," "Maeve," "Maria," "Mary," "Danielle," "Leslie," "Mark," and "Chris."

Enormous appreciation is also due to my sex gurus, Becca Brewer and Catherine Rose.

To Jennifer Margulis and Krista Klein and Sarah Madgic and Laura Purpura and Kelly Corrigan, my thanks for reading draft after draft. But more importantly, my thanks for the friendship and support that is even more important to me than your incomparable judgment.

To my agent, Jennifer de la Fuente, and my editor,

Elizabeth Beier—how much fun has this been?! I could not have asked for more from either of you.

To Mom and Dad and especially to Ellis . . . thank you thank you thank you . . . for who you are and how that makes me who I am.

And finally . . . my love and devotion and appreciation and adoration and respect and indebtedness especially to my kids . . . and to Bill.